Bulletproof

A Cop's Guide to Financial Success

Brett M. Ward

AuthorHouse™
1663 Liberty Drive, Suite 200
Bloomington, IN 47403
www.authorhouse.com
Phone: 1-800-839-8640

AuthorHouse™ UK Ltd.
500 Avebury Boulevard
Central Milton Keynes, MK9 2BE
www.authorhouse.co.uk
Phone: 08001974150

© 2007 Brett M. Ward. All rights reserved.

No part of this book may be reproduced, stored in a retrieval system, or transmitted by any means without the written permission of the author.

First published by AuthorHouse 11/28/2007

ISBN: 978-1-4343-4749-7 (e)
ISBN: 978-1-4259-9271-2 (sc)

Library of Congress Control Number: 2007901023

Printed in the United States of America
Bloomington, Indiana

This book is printed on acid-free paper.

Dedication

This book could never have become a reality, nor anything within accomplished without the complete and unwavering support of my mom, Barbara Marie Ward. Although she passed away before reading this son's book in print, she lived to see all her sons succeed.

I wish to also thank my nephew, Ryan Raymond Ward, whose dedication to this book project has made all the difference.

Table of Contents

Foreword ix
Introduction xiii
Commonly Asked Questions 1
Getting Started 11
Budgeting/Expense Management 25
Credit/Debit 33
Investing 101 41
Scenarios 53
Over the Top: Extreme Saving Tips 71
Synergism in Partnership 83
Retirement to Pension: A Look Back from
    2003 to 2006 89
Bringing It All Together: Essential Points 105
Epilogue 119

Foreword

It is my hope that you give the ideas and suggestions in the following pages a chance in your life. Though each one of us walks a unique path through the years of a career, the commonality of our profession bears, I believe, heavily on this book's relevance and its ability to help you retire successfully ... at a young age.

I wish to make mention, at this early juncture, of my friend and former colleague, David M. Rieumont, whose name you can expect to see during the course of this book. Besides friendship, David Rieumont provided to me, and to all who knew him, support and guidance through our years together in law enforcement.

By sheer chance and circumstance, David and I wound up at exactly the same police academy and department, served an almost identical number of years, and retired at exactly the same age (forty-three and a half).

The closeness of our ideas regarding finances, and thus how we each conducted our business, revealed to me how powerful this book's message really is. Through my friendship with David and seeing for myself in another the discipline I had mastered at work provided an incredibly powerful dose of confidence. For that, I am deeply indebted to my friend.

Something else I wish to convey to you is that I am certain this guide is not the only roadmap to success.

Whenever you can build further on these ideas, or find the inspiration for new ones, you should absolutely do so. Just knowing you are now of the mindset to succeed outside the parameters of law enforcement is a giant step forward. Feel free to get as creative as you like. Brainstorm with others and ask questions.

Remember as you read this book that all of the material herein is based on research/information and personal experience. It is my hope that with this easy-to-read, narrative-style book that I have tied together in brevity but with substance, twenty years of financial planning, focusing on you: the law enforcement professional.

In this ever-changing and increasingly challenging world, I have concluded that there is simply never too much we can do for ourselves when trying to ensure our financial security. I have always used the phrase "taking the edge off" when trying to either chip away at some expense or face a challenge. Each day, every day, if we can win those little battles—save on this, use less of that, put away a bit more than the day before—over the course of time, then, it must follow that we will win the war. You will notice the difference and you will see the results. It's no different than in your marksmanship or first aid, or any other type of training: You must learn or relearn the techniques, apply them, and remember: "Practice makes perfect."

"Every battle is won before it's ever fought."

Sun-Tsu — ***The Art of War***

Introduction

As I sit here penning this introduction, a cool breeze wafts toward me from the balcony of my condo. It's 3:55 PM, and I am home for the day after a quiet forty-five-minute shift at my post as a crossing guard. I am forty-eight years of age, but I retired from full-time work as a police officer four and a half years ago, in 2003, at age forty-three.

My former academy mate and friend David Rieumont retired from our department as well, in 2004, and has since launched a very successful second career as both a licensed charter boat captain and radio talk show co-host. What is striking, however, is that both of us successfully left law enforcement—financially secure—in our early forties.

David and I attended the Pinellas Police Academy in the spring of 1984, "put our time in" on the job, and did what very few others around us in law enforcement could do: Leave exactly when we wanted, with no regrets or worries.

The motivation in writing this book, for me, is rooted in the firsthand knowledge we have of just how demanding law enforcement is, and how twenty years on this job equals easily thirty years in average "non-hazardous" positions.

By the way, thirty years service *does* constitute a full-term career in other positions. This, and the genuine desire to help my brother and sister officers in an area I believe is completely ignored both in academy training and throughout the span of the officer's career: financial planning, which

I hope will help you as it helped me in planning that last shift.

Until I can have my guide included on police academy and departmental reading lists, I must settle for reaching those of you who were curious enough to purchase this book. I assure you, reader, you have made a wise choice.

Much of the advice offered herein may seem a mixture of the unorthodox, the old-fashioned, no fun, or even odd. Rest assured, it is all of this and more. But also, it is powerful stuff that has been tested, and it works.

For example, in the fall of 2003, it came time, I decided, to part with my 1993 Ford Mustang after it had provided me with ten-plus years of reliable service. Offered at five hundred dollars, it was a fair deal for my buyer.

I had always taken very good care of my car, and the replaced parts alone were worth twice the asking price. The point, though, is that three people I know expressed immediate interest in purchasing the car. Rather than mentioning names and causing them undue embarrassment, suffice it to say that this group of potential buyers included a deputy sheriff, a college student, and a career air force sergeant.

To ensure that I do not come across wrong, I wish to point out that all of these people are within my circle, and are good people. Sadly, though, not one of them had five hundred dollars put together to make the buy. Furthermore, it turned out to be the college student who bought my car after all.

By now I am sure you know where I am going with this… It was shocking to learn that anyone could be in this incredibly expensive, modern world and actually not have access to just five hundred dollars! Okay, I admit I have been told that my way of looking at money—if not at life—is a bit unusual. Thank you. Because in my words you'll find the blended teachings of both the great and common people I have both studied and known personally. Everyone from Donald Trump to my own grandfather has had an important role in shaping my financial ethos. I hope my own touch in passing these lessons on to you helps you and proves to be enjoyable reading at the same time.

My own motto, to the amusement of others is "Live like a monk, save like a madman." For the ten years I planned my escape, I set aside between 45 and 55 percent of my *net* income. That, along with placing myself on a strict budget and investment plan, got me just where I wanted to be—on that balcony early in the afternoon, done for the day, or for a lifetime if I chose.

In summary, you will find chapters herein that touch upon everything you will need in order to plan your escape, with sage step-by-step tips on how to get there. Welcome to my world and good luck .... I will be looking for you out on that balcony!

Commonly Asked Questions

Why should I read this book?

Anyone who works in law enforcement in this country automatically shares a bond with the author. I have completed a career as a police officer, and because of this, I can relate to you personally, financially, and emotionally. I have a basic familiarity with its salary structure; the common threads of a career in police work, i.e. the concerns and needs that officers commonly have. Most of all, I did it.

I made it to retirement and got out young. I believe that this "peek" back as to how I managed this will prove invaluable to you as an example. Just as retired professional athletes return to offer sports camps, or how retired CEOs go on 25K-a-pop speaking tours, here I am. What I want is to help you in a field that is simply overlooked in training. That is why you should read this book.

About the author — What do I know about him, and why should I take his advice?

I spent nineteen years in law enforcement, attending the police academy in 1984 and retiring honorably in 2003. I hold a bachelor's degree in criminology from St. Leo University (Florida) and have done graduate work at the University of

South Florida. My entire career was spent as a patrol officer, with many specialized training accreditations having been earned. I am also a United States Coast Guard licensed captain. The best legacy I ever could hope for is to offer advice to future officers that helps fill a gap which I know exists.

Recently, I have met with an ex-lieutenant of mine who now heads the training department at the local police academy. I mentioned this book and its ideas to him, and Lieutenant Byrd responded quite enthusiastically. My hope is to have this guide added to police academy reading lists. The advice worked for me, it worked for David, and it will work for you.

Can this book work for me?

This book would prove useful to anyone in the American workforce, but because I am comfortable addressing a law enforcement audience, and because police work is where my heart is, I targeted you, my brother and sister officers.

And why not? Don't doctors routinely extend professional courtesies to other doctors? Stock tips, too, are routinely traded back and forth among brokers. CEOs do more business on golf courses than in boardrooms.

Police officers, meanwhile, are out there in the cold when it comes to such valuable information and courtesies. There just does not seem to be anyone clamoring to counsel the men and women who night after night put their lives on the line in a field that is not too well-paid and oftentimes not appreciated.

If I have specific questions, can the author be contacted?

As far as I am concerned, you may contact me; however, as this is my first venture into book writing, you will most likely have to go through the publisher, as they handle marketing, appearances, and publicity. Because I am a retired police officer, I must be conscious of personal safety issues, but I want other officers to feel I am here for you; so I plan to address this with the publisher.

Let me say that, as far as the advice in my book, some tips and strategies were delivered in broad strokes; but I did try to spend time on a cross-section of financial issues, which I hope will help. Feel free to forward any questions or comments to the address provided by the publishing company. You have my word, I will respond when applicable.

Will the advice in this book change my life?

It sure has shaped my life, and David's too. If you are diligent in applying just one suggestion I have offered, I am certain that things will improve for you. That is a given. The degree and scope of the improvement in your life depends only on you and how closely and faithfully you commit yourself. I am confident that you will be amazed at the changes in how you look at things, and surprised at how the career you have chosen can be molded into one that brings financial success, despite being paid an average salary.

When executed well, over the course of years, you may find you will become wealthy. You have much greater control of your life than imaginable; all of us do. Speaking of financial matters, once you establish a budget and begin really paying attention to where your money is going, you are going to find that changes will come naturally. Stay ahead with everything: bills, plans, and dreams. Believe me, upward mobility is attainable for the average street cop.

Can I really make the changes asked of me?

The only answer to this question is that it is up to you and you alone. This guide does not apply equally to everyone in every situation. Sure, there is no way the guy with five kids can normally put away as much money as the single rookie living at home. But can that same father of five benefit greatly by managing to slice 100 or 200 dollars a month off his bills in some way? Sure. The closer you look, the more you will find ways to cut and ways to save.

No form of change is easy at first. Humans are creatures of habit, cops especially so. The nature of the job dictates that we follow standard operating or routine procedures. Indeed, the adherence to such procedures keeps us alive. Now, financially speaking, my job is to break you of your bad habits. That is my mission, to put more of your money back in your pockets and expose those habits that cause your money to leave you in the first place.

Is there any room for error or compromise?

If there was no room for compromise and error, then neither David nor I nor anyone would ever have hope for success. Life is filled with mistakes, shortfalls, misfortunes, and even tragedies. You must try to keep the error list as short as possible; over that, you have control. Sure, we all blow it from time to time. All this means is that you will have to work a bit harder, nothing more. It does not necessarily exempt you from financial success. Compromises, well, these are a must; they are what this book rests on. You want a brand-new car? Fine. Go out and get it; but then take care of it and keep it for ten years. A new home? Sure, this is most likely a great investment. Do it right, though. Shop for a good mortgage rate, buy well, and always pay down the principal. The whole idea of this book is to correct bad financial behavior and to teach *internal compromise* and *delayed gratification*.

As time goes by, you will find that the number of mistakes that slip by unnoticed will lessen. Also, the number of compromises you will have to make will shrink, the more you get ahead.

How can this book apply to everyone?

Simply because regarding everything in life, we are all in the same boat. Essentially, all of us want the same things: security for ourselves and for our loved ones, and the freedom to live our life as we see fit. This book will bring you closer to financial freedom, which will empower you to choose what you do. What is said in these pages works; the only limitations are your level of commitment.

Time is the most important concept in this book. Just basic numbers prove that; $15,000 saved each year over a three-year period equals $45,000. After managing to put away that same $15,000 each year for ten years, without interest, you would have $150,000.

Before you purchase this book, borrow one, and if it would make you more certain of its merit, take it to any certified financial planner for a review. Please. Because I am that sure you will get a thumbs-up. Be warned, however, you may not get the book back! I have to pass on a true story of an experience David related to me about an encounter he once had with a certified financial planner he once consulted. After the customary introductions, David surprised the C.F.P. with personal inquiries about the C.F.P.'s own level of financial assets and security. He asked to see the C.F.P.'s portfolio, and the flabbergasted consultant politely but steadfastly declined.

As it turns out, the C.F.P. eventually admitted to having only a small amount of net worth. She assured David, though, that she could be of service to him. David packed up his papers, thanked the C.F.P. for her time, and said goodbye. Just like Lance Armstrong said in his famous book, "It's Not About the Bike."

Anyone can succeed and anyone can fail. As I explained earlier, I chose to direct this guide to the law enforcement audience because I walked in your shoes. Police work, including basic pay scales and benefits, is essentially similar, no matter where you happen to work. Sure, officers in major cities earn more than officers in rural towns, but then the price for home sales in rural America is not a thousand dollars per square foot, like it is in New York City. Everything is relative, but anyone can benefit from good advice.

What is this book *not* designed to do?

Okay, in order to give you an honest answer to this question, I must talk tough. Look at this as "tough love." This book's only promise is that by following any of my advice, you will better your balance sheet, enough to notice and to make a difference. Now that we have gotten that out of the way, sadly, some readers may find themselves just simply too far gone financially to ever be able to really get ahead. Multiple costly divorces, serious illness, years of flagrantly irresponsible financial behavior—the list goes on. These are very hard to overcome, for anyone. This book requires a long-term commitment to change, and attention to preparing for the future, rather than indulging in the moment. Remember the concept of *time* being mentioned and that as the saying goes, "Rome was not built in a day."

I have to include one good example of how this book is useless to anyone with unrealistic expectations.... I have a friend who is a detective with the department I retired from. Upon hearing about the nature of my book, she was excited about reading it, because she needed a few tips! It seems Jane D. had recently gone through a breakup, and felt she had better get back on track, since she now found herself on her own. Disappointed in her reasoning but flattered she was interested in my work, I promised her a signed copy. Folks, this will not help anyone with such a mindset. This is not a six-week summer makeover. It is not a sexy way of life, and most of all, it is not a magic bullet. Followed closely, however, I promise you this book will not let you down if you apply it. The advice herein will lead you to a better life over time.

Will the advice that's given become outdated, or is this guide something I can always refer back to?

Without a doubt, the core ideas offered herein are timeless. How could such advice as to live within your means, prepare for your future, and work hard toward a worthwhile goal ever become obsolete? This book addresses what life is all about, what we are all trying to do ... secure a future for ourselves. If each one of us improves ourselves financially, society as a whole improves. Credit card debt, for one thing, is crippling America. If we bring debt down, then spendable income will increase. I wish to include three independent newspaper articles in the book, because they appeared in my local newspaper at such an opportune time (near the book's completion).

The article below, "Florida's Nest Egg Neglect" appeared on September 7, 2006, in the *Insider* section of the *St. Petersburg Times*. The article addresses different

Florida cities' ranking among 500 U.S. cities as far as "nest egg" e.g. retirement savings. Of course, I am concerned that the other forty-nine states address saving as well. I live in Florida, however, and have no idea how far an audience this book will reach. So I included the article for my Florida readers.

FLORIDIA NEST EGG NEGLECT

If your nest egg is puny, you may not be able to retire, but at least you'll have lots of company. The Tampa Bay area isn't just below average nationally, it's among the worst in the state for nurturing nest eggs. That's the verdict from brokerage firm A.G. Edwards, which released its second annual Nest Egg Index on Wednesday. The index is based on factors such as personal savings rates, household wealth, home ownership, cost of living, unemployment rate and retirement plan penetration. For more on how the states rank or to comment on the results, go to Times Personal Finance editor Helen Huntley's Money Talk blog at **blogs.tampabay.com/money**

How Florida communities' saving and investing habits stack up. The number is their ranking out of 500 communities nationwide in A.G. Edwards' Nest Egg Index.

- **15.** Naples-Marco Island
- **83.** Palm Coast
- **106.** Sarasota-Bradenton
- **121.** Punta Gorda
- **135.** Fort Myers-Cape Coral
- **139.** Vero Beach
- **185.** Key West-Marathon
- **213.** Fort Pierce-Port St. Lucie
- **246.** Melbourne-Titusville-Palm Bay
- **270.** The Villages
- **351.** Homosassa Springs
- **356.** Jacksonville
- **366.** Daytona Beach-Deltona-Ormond Beach
- **367.** Orlando
- **379.** Tampa-St. Petersburg-Clearwater
- **463.** Ocala
- **470.** Pensacola-Ferry Bass-Brent
- **471.** Miami-Fort Lauderdale-Miam Beach

Good ideas are good now and always. Some of the prices, figures, and other technical information will change, but this will not affect what is important. When you have finished this book, you will be sufficiently armed for battle in that ever-so-important financial arena. And the words of Sun-Tsu in The Art of War again will prove correct: "Every battle is won before it's ever fought." Good Luck.

Getting Started

Before editing, I had this chapter geared toward the police recruit and rookie officer, and I suppose a great percentage of my reading audience may fall into these groups, should this book be included on academy reading lists. Thinking about it, though, it occurred to me that it really does not matter which officer, junior or senior, picks up this guide, because everyone will be commencing on the same journey.

Your first order of business is to acquire the forms from your payroll department for a 457K sign up. In layman's terms, the 457K is the government employee's version of a 401K. Police officers, being public servants, are prohibited from participating in 401Ks, but both offer the participant similar benefits. The 457K allows officers to set aside a certain percentage of their gross earnings in a tax-deferred account. Taxes are not paid on your contributions until you finally draw on it, which is when—and not until—you eventually separate from your city employer. Also, the maximum annual amount you may lay aside in a 457K is capped and regulated by Congress. Generally, the cap is raised every year (or couple of years), and I believe it's currently $15,500 per year. (Note: get accurate figures from your city payroll department. Since severing my contributions, I have not followed the plan.) The point is that the amount you contribute comes off the top of your taxable income; so if you earn $45,000 a year and contribute $12,000 to a 457K, then, for tax purposes, your income was only $33,000. In my case, I began contribution to a 457K plan in 1997, only with the goal of establishing a "side" investment. At first, my level of contribution was lower, maybe just $5,000 or so a year; but as my salary rose, I boosted those levels to the maximum allowed. When I separated (retired) from the City of Clearwater in 2003, I remember having amassed about $45,000 in savings.

That story is noteworthy for two reasons: first, for the prior twelve years I had been employed in my department, I never knew such a fund existed. Like so many of my comrades, I was concerned with all things policework related, not some obscure government tax plan. This, in retrospect, was crippling; and it's things like this that motivated me to write this book. If someone had sat me down, forced me to listen and digest the information on a 457K, and pushed me to enroll, I would have retired with easily $100,000 more in my account than I had. Spread over twelve years, with all my raises, overtime, and off-duty work, the $100,000 would have not been missed too much. True, even after enrolling, I did not start at maximum levels, but that was because I was pouring thousands each year into more traditional, liquid investments.

So begin at levels you can tolerate, but be aware of your structured raises, overtime availability, etc., because these extras give you the chance to boost your levels without ever feeling the pinch. My rule has always been save until it hurts, then save a bit more! I have always made a game out of saving; here's how: One rule I have is that if ever I decide to take money out of any of my savings/investments (no matter the reason), it's treated as a loan that's owed, with interest. No kidding. Of course, in a 457K fund, that wouldn't apply because barring an emergency, you cannot pull from those funds. In deciding what percentage of your money to allocate to a 457K, you must remember this. Anyway, back to the loan idea; this practice will prove extremely effective in both keeping you reluctant toward tapping into savings, and put you even further ahead, should you borrow. I charged myself 20 percent on any loan; so if I borrowed $1,000, when I repaid the loan, my account read $1,200! Over the course of time, games and practices like this will become second nature to you; and they work. This kind of advice goes to the central theme of this guide: It takes a change in behavior and attitude to begin moving toward financial success. Even if you believe yourself to be in a bad financial position, I promise that if you adhere to the advice I give you, your situation will take an important turn for the better.

For me, I hope to reach, through this book, those who want the guidance. I have made it clear to the publisher, and to interested marketing firms, that I don't want to force myself on others through aggressive promoting and advertising campaigns. Pouring my heart into this product and then simply offering it up to you is, I believe, my end of the bargain. Your end, by choice, is to read on and give the ideas herein a chance. All of us live together in this complicated, modern world, and we all fall victim to its temptations—material and otherwise. Ironically, though, those best served, in one sense, by this guide are those who have made the worst mistakes. Any worthwhile guidance here will ease that bad situation more noticeably than it would those already doing well.

Also, no matter where you are in your career, you can jump right in with this program. Regarding 457K funds, generally, if you are a rookie who probably faces large purchases in the near future (home, car, etc.), dividing your disposable income becomes important. You must have enough liquid funds for such purchases. Of course, if you are married, this gives you greater leeway in your allocation. Even if your salary is weighted rather heavily in the 457K, you can still fall back on your spouse's income for support. Understand that while it is impossible to address every scenario in people's lives, we do share an important commonality, in that we all work (or have worked) in law enforcement. I did devote, however, an entire chapter to scenarios, so you may thumb to the particular example that best fits you.

The officer who is married, with a family, and needs a larger, more expensive house will not be able to devote as much to actual savings and investment; but my message is that "that's okay," because real estate is generally a great investment. And such purchases fit, too, into a sound financial plan. Regarding whether or not this guide is for you, the answer will come to you soon. This plan takes staying power, and the ability to embrace that old economics phrase "delayed gratification." You will need to keep a smile in the face of skepticism and even ridicule, and learn to do things the "good old-fashioned way"! You will have to make tough choices; but know this: The rewards are great. To quote a line from the movie *Wall Street*, Charlie Sheen's character Budd Fox had it right when he said, "There is no nobility in poverty anymore." What you do with your money and success is what's all-important. One example is Bill Gates, one of the wealthiest people on earth. Mr. Gates has pledged to begin donating his fortune, in a structured payout, so as to be completely donated by the time of his death. This says clearly that one does not have to be poor to be nice. I'm sorry, but generally I see around me a resentment of the "haves" by the "have-nots." Nothing new, I guess, except that we have a choice here in America (and in this career) of which group we belong to.

Government is coming to realize that the better the individual citizen fares, so too, is society buoyed. Greater income means greater spending power. Education, generally tied somewhat to financial success, has become a core campaign priority in every election. People everywhere are being encouraged to save more, to think ahead. It's my hope that this guide takes this concept a bit further.

Your second simultaneous task in getting started, but of equal importance to a 457K, is to get a bearing on where your balance sheet stands. To do this, start with two columns: Income and Expenses. Plainly and simply, begin listing each and every item on both sides. Naturally the "income" side will be rather straightforward; but should you be married, or have two or more jobs, list all here. For now, though, leave out overtime or off-duty income (even if your department assigns permanent off-duty jobs). I will get back to these extras later. Regarding income, list your *net* income, because after all, this is what you have to work with.

Now, for the expenses: Compile an honest, detailed list of just what you pay toward every month. You must be thorough in this column, because it is this group that drags your income column down like a weight, and here is where we must adjust. The following is a sample list of common monthly expenses. Take those which apply to your budget, and adjust as applicable.

- **Mortgage/rent**
- **Power bill**
- **Water, garbage collection**
- **Telephone (excluding cellular)**
- **Cable/satellite TV**
- **Internet fees (if applicable)**
- **Food**
- **Insurance—Auto, homeowners, life , health, dental, vision**
- **Newspaper/magazine subscriptions**
- **Haircuts/personal hygiene**

- **Vehicle maintenance/gasoline**
- **Travel expenses**
- **Entertainment**
- **Credit/charge cards**
- **Miscellaneous**
- **Emergency**

This expense list is where the "buck" both starts and ends. It represents the key ingredient in your recipe for financial success. After you have filled it out completely, compare the totals of both columns and note the difference in dollar amounts.

Assuming you are in the black, giving you disposable income, you are ready to start saving and investing. Still, you must work hard at bringing down the expense total. It is not enough to simply find that you have extra money available at the month's end. In fact, if you have the same experience that I had, the first time you compile such a list, you will be astonished at just how much money is going out, and to how many places it's going. In my case, this prompted me to pause and reflect on how I could cut from that expense monstrosity. I am hoping it will have the same effect on you.

God forbid you are in the red each month, this juncture of "slice and dice" becomes critical. You must find areas you can cut from, just as in government. This is never easy and never really fun. I must emphasize, too, that I believe everyone should plan to periodically tweak these figures. Both as income rises, and to even perhaps have money for new expenses, should they arrive. The financial world is ever fluid with an almost-constant ebb and flow, just as you should be.

In each of our lives, dozens of seldom-paid-attention-to little expenses slip through the cracks; but when totaled, they add up to often sizeable sums. Just by switching my car insurance company, I saved $280 per year in premiums. Although that doesn't sound like much, over ten years, that's $2,800. In the book, *The Millionaire Next Door*, I read that almost no one who belongs to that club would stand out in a crowd. These folks lead ordinary lives, and yet they are set for life.

Okay, now that you have managed to drive your outlay column down, the scale should begin to tip toward that much extra income. If you recall, I had you purposely omit any overtime, extra-duty-type earnings from your income column. The reason is twofold: First, you should never base your monthly available cash figure on an extra, such as overtime. I actually know someone who had to secure a letter from his boss, wherein he was guaranteed a certain amount of overtime each month. Evidently, my friend required a higher income figure in order to qualify for a mortgage. When I heard of this, I was mortified. Good God, would you really want to put yourself in such a position? What happens if the overtime somehow dried up? Or as we all do, if Bruce got older and tired?

Never put yourself behind the eight ball if you can avoid it. The second reason to keep overtime outside the figuring is if you do work it, make it count—toward investing/saving, not toward bills. The quickest way to lose your drive is to get that feeling that you can't see the fruits of your labor. Every penny of my overtime was put into play in the market, because I gave up my holidays, evenings, and weekends working these details. Something else you must avoid is allowing your money to be too accessible to you. Don't keep much in your wallet, and structure your accounts so that you must sign for the funds, by U.S. Mail versus just by phone. If you develop the ability to always save money, you will never stay down for long.

After my divorce in 1993, I left with $3,000 to my name. But I had faith in myself and in my ability to rebound. I got started immediately, saving $1,000 to $2,000 each time. I set upon building a fund base with my mom being the keeper of my savings. Each time I reached that amount, my mom advised me of such, and I started opening mutual funds and buying stocks. I built an initial portfolio of nine funds. Once they were established, I poured additional investment money into each one of them. Whenever I invested in a particular fund, that stock or mutual fund went to the bottom of the pile. Before I knew it, my portfolio was over $15,000 and growing rapidly. Aside from the bull market of the late 1990s, I was working more and more extra duty jobs. At one point, I tried actually investing my entire regular salary and living on my overtime money.

The old adage "money makes money" is very true. One example worth noting is of a particular bank stock I had begun investing in. I bought consistently up from the mid-teens to $66. When the stock hit $66 per share, it split (2 for 1) to $33 of course—but at that price, the stock became affordable once again. The stock rose again, doubling my holdings, this time to $76 per share... at which time I sold. By then, I had several hundred shares, and with my profits, I took my mom on an Alaskan cruise, redecorated my bedroom with antique cherrywood furniture, purchased furniture for my mom, and then reinvested a ton of money back in the market and elsewhere. Sure, my own money (the principal, if you will) worked for me in this stock purchase regimen, but in actuality, the bulk of my profits came from motivators both within the stock itself and in such a great market. As the stock rose in price, all I really had to do was stay on automatic pilot and keep buying. The rest was easy: Just watch a great company keep doing the right thing, and cash out when it hit Pluto.

Critics, of course, will seize upon this opportunity to blast me, saying, "Okay, fine in that case, but the stock could have lost value." They would be quite right; but then your buy-in price tag would be lower. With the same amount of money (say $500), if a stock price dips from $50 per share to $40, then instead of purchasing just 10 shares (with $500) you would then purchase 12.5 shares. Working with that dollar amount, the impact of *dollar cost averaging*, which is what that's known as, is not as dramatic as with a $20,000 purchase

Bulletproof

of that same $50 stock. With a ten-dollar drop in price, you then would acquire an additional one hundred shares.

Another point you must remember in reading stock prices is that a drop in price represents only a loss on paper unless you sell. Panic buying or selling is never advisable. Give the stock time to rebound; usually it will. If by year's end it has not, and you need a tax break, dump that lagging stock; you can write off (deduct) your losses with the IRS.

With regard to getting started, you will find that most, if not all, of your expenses can be cut. Avoiding name brands, extra unnecessary features on cell phones or cable service, and upscale stores can shave hundreds off your expenses column. Stocks and mutual funds can oftentimes be purchased directly, without the need of a broker. Additional purchases and redemptions can be made via U.S. Mail, all of which keeps more of your money, your money, by avoiding broker fees/ commissions. Always reinvest your dividends. *Dividends* are monies paid out, sometimes quarterly or otherwise, which can either be paid to you by check or applied to the purchase of more stock. Until your dividends become substantial, these payout amounts will only buy you fractional shares. Over time, with consistent investing, however, your stock portfolio's value will grow. I have heard that the average annual gain in the stock market since the 1929 crash has been roughly 12 percent. We have a strong economy, still the most powerful on earth. And markets tend to be cyclical. Once you realize this, these natural upturns and downturns won't rattle you so much.

Timing when you retire, if you are heavily invested, is very important. Of course, it is impossible to predict what the market will do, but if you are ready to pull the pin, and your 457K fund is at a fifty-two-week high, it may be an opportune time to "take your money and run." I remember some stories of officers on my department who planned their retirement for late 2001 or early 2002 and went ahead with it; they took a beating in their payout figure because of the incredible drop in market levels after 9/11. Fortunately for me, by 2003, the markets had been in an upturn for some time. Still, my fund had not gotten back completely to pre-9/11 level.

I felt the time was at hand for me to retire; economics was not at the center of my decision. For all of you getting started in your career, be advised—twenty years, give or take—that is what you have got. Use them well, for in one sense, that's a long time, but looking back, they went by in a flash. I shared with the publisher that I wanted this book priced affordably, and hope you believe it was. The true measure of the book's value, though, will be the extent to which it helps you: what you take from it. Even though you may only be getting started in law enforcement, this guide will help you in getting started properly. Police work is unique because for one thing, the nature of the job tends to isolate us from many facets of society.

We work odd hours, deal with stressful and critical situations constantly, and we are held to a much higher standard than the average citizen. Police work is definitely a calling, but we must realize that we still belong to the outside economic world in which we live. Therefore, we must prepare for what's next and begin doing so immediately. With the lessons of this guide added to your arsenal, I believe you will have the financial ammunition you need to better your life both while "on the job" and afterward.

Budgeting/Expense Management

In my chapter "Commonly Asked Questions," I referred to a St. Petersburg Times newspaper article to highlight the finding that Floridians, along with citizens in all other forty-nine states, generally are behind in their "nest egg savings." At the risk of appearing to focus on negativity, I must include a second article from the *St. Petersburg Times* which appeared on the very same date; also in the *Insider* section (September 7, 2006, p. 1). The article, titled "Cost Increases" consists of a graph reflecting the changes in prices in consumables from July 2005 to July 2006, based on the consumer price index. The figures were pulled from data compiled by the Bureau of Labor Statistics.

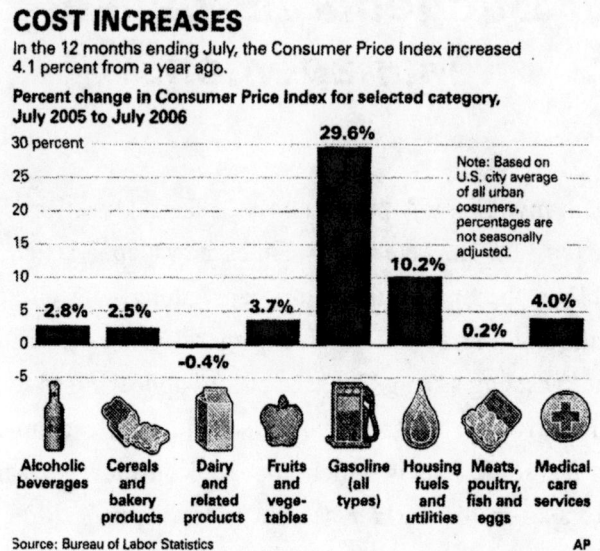

This informative chart bears directly on the importance of this chapter's message: to cut costs for yourself wherever and whenever and however you can. Again, the timing of such an article, with such valuable information, could not have been better for purposes of this book. Unfortunately, the data is rather alarming. It seems as if only one category dropped in overall cost over the past twelve months, whereas seven others rose, at an average of 4.1 percent. On another note, I remind you that my pension has but a 1.5 percent annual C.O.L.A. built in, which means that based on the figures, I fell 2.6 percent behind rising costs, in a one-year period . I do not have figures available regarding pay increases in my former department for active officers, but memory tells me that the average yearly raise is about 5 percent. That would bring the officer just .9 percent ahead.

Since this essentially means that the individual is breaking even, it becomes so much more vital that we all cut down expenses where we can.

Before this article appeared, I had this chapter already written, but I believe I can serve you better by going back and looking closely at each area of notation, since this article appears to address most of our everyday consumables.

Alcoholic Beverages - The only such beverage I purchase is wine, for cooking, so it is hard for me to say too much more on this product. At 2.8 percent, the increase in cost seems relatively low. I recommend shopping for savings in every aisle of the liquor store, however. Do what you can here.

Cereals and Bakery Products - Up 2.5 percent, again not bad. I can tell you though that to this day, I still pay $1.25 for a fresh loaf of flavored bread at a major supermarket. In that same store, other "artesian" bread goes for upwards of $3. Many major supermarkets offer "two-for-one" sales. Even if the price of the initial item may be higher than elsewhere, when you add the second item for free, the average price comes way down. Again, stay away from name brands; shop at discount stores, and where you can, buy in bulk.

Fruits and Vegetables - Although up 3.7 percent, we cannot afford health-wise to forgo this food group. Studies have proven beyond doubt that eating right is essential. Cost-wise, too, it is a lot cheaper to maintain one's health than to pay outrageous hospital bills, which illness and disease bring. Remember, "An ounce of prevention is worth a pound of cure."

Brett Michael Ward

Gasoline - I know I addressed this elsewhere, but the chance to take a few more shots at this behemoth of an issue is just too compelling to forgo at 29.6 percent. I would have guessed more, but figures (I hope) do not lie. Aside from being an utterly crippling burden for American motorists to bear, these costs and increases should be deemed illegal. During natural disasters, I find it ironic and sardonically humorous how ads appear on TV addressing laws going into effect regarding price gouging. We are being price gouged on a daily basis, all over the country, at these fuel cost levels. Government must address this, because otherwise, the effects will ripple into every realm of private budgeting, with serious consequences. Imagine the worker facing a decision of buying food or fueling up (so he or she can get to work, which essentially keeps America running). Tax dollars, salaries for elected officials, infrastructure, defense allocation, *everything* depends on the American workforce getting to work. 29.6 percent. Looking at the chart, that is 19.4 percent higher than the second-most-inflationary consumable.

Aside from being a finite resource, oil is controlled (for the most part) by an entity known as OPEC. We can no longer permit ourselves to linger in a perpetual state of check by relying so heavily on any one product. Fortunately, hybrid vehicles and alternative fuel sources are being developed. As with any new technologies, however, there is a lag time which is inevitable and oftentimes protracted. Meanwhile, until the technology can be perfected, the fuel crisis worsens.

It is not surprising that the second-highest percentage gain in a consumable is heating fuels and utilities—oil again rears its ugly head. True, many homes are heated by natural gas or by electricity, but these types of energy sources are included in that 10.2 percent average increase. Cut costs in any possible way—by purchasing economical vehicles, turning off unused lights, etc. Look closely at everything.

Meats, Poultry, Fish, and Eggs -   0.2 percent. I am almost speechless. This is an increase we can live with. In addition, fish and eggs are products considered good for you. Not that meats and poultry are not, but they rest higher on the food pyramid than do fish, vegetables and fruits, and other items. Buy wisely, no matter: Where you shop matters as much or more as what you buy.

Medical Care Services - Although the phrasing of this category seems ambiguous, I have to assume it includes health care. If so, I'm astonished that the rise in costs over any twelve-month period is just 4.0 percent. My own health care policy has seen more than a 10 percent hike in the past year—despite my being a non-smoker, non-drinker, with no pre-existing medical conditions. Even with just a 4.0 percent rise; according to a recent study by *Families USA*, 89.6 million individuals (over 70 percent of whom were employed full-time) lacked health insurance in the U.S. in 2006 (*St. Petersburg Times*, *Nation*, Fri. Sept. 21, 2007 P. 3A). That is a fact.

The figure (4.0 percent) although probably correct, I would guess fails to take into account that costs were already at very high levels— something like increasing one's vehicle speed from 95 mph to 100 mph. Although the 5-mph change is very little, the initial 40 mph over the speed limit is concerning.

Another thing to consider when studying this increase is that we are not provided any previous years' data in the graph. Multiplied (at the same 4.0 percent rate) the figure jumps to a 20 percent rise in consumer costs over just a five-year period. (In five years, C.O.L.A. would provide a 7.5 percent raise, leaving me 12.5 percent in the red.) You have to think in these terms, and sit down frequently to re-address your outlays.

In my world, there is no place for mortgages, car payments, fuel-guzzling vehicles, or waste of any sort.

The category of *Entertainment* was not included in the chart of consumables, and I think it ought to have been. True, it is essentially an intangible, but nevertheless, it is a product we all need in our lives. To me, the cost of one of this country's biggest forms of entertainment—the big screen—has risen to unacceptable levels. In my area, over the past ten years, theaters with bottom-dollar admission prices have virtually vanished. Fortunately, a few remain in the form of "Cinema Draft houses." Do not be fooled by the name, however; these are not the beer-flowing, wild establishments of old.

"Cinema Draft houses" offer the same movies as first-run theaters do, but after the movies have already made the initial runs (at the initial high prices). Whether you are viewing *Titanic, Saving Private Ryan,* or *World Trade*

Center for the first time in August or that coming December, the experience will be exactly the same.

"Cinema Draft houses" offer great admission prices, and typically offer great food at average prices. Of course, the value lies in the savings in your admission costs. Movie theaters, I believe, do not have to charge so much for admission. Most (if not all) do sell food, which in itself provides a great profit margin and ensures overall profit for the establishment. Many other forms of entertainment are just simply an essential part of American life, and thus an important part of our lives. Mickey Mouse's ears are the single most recognizable symbol in the world—that is also a fact.

It behooves such great American establishments (such as Disney World/Disneyland) to preserve the affordability and thus accessibility for American families. Sadly, I think it is safe to say that more and more in America is becoming out of reach for many folks.

So then, in closing, I have introduced scientific data (which I hope has been kept to tolerable levels) in order to illustrate my position that generally speaking, we are falling behind (or at least losing ground) because of burgeoning costs all around us. Although public awareness of these inflationary areas is broadening, I believe that this problem can only be fixed if it is recognized. So much goes unnoticed in our daily life, and we have little time to compare and evaluate every purchase we make.

Brett Michael Ward

Kudos to the Bureau of Labor Statistics for shining their spotlight on cost increases. The same goes for my local newspaper, The *St. Petersburg Times*, which ran an article titled "Wal-Mart's $4 drug plan goes statewide: The company also expands the list of medicines available in the program. Target matches the offer" (October 6, 2006 front page *St. Petersburg Times*). Of course, most of all, thanks to Wal-Mart for their abiding goal of providing us, their consumers and neighbors, with these essential products at affordable prices. Companies such as this enable Americans to successfully budget and manage our expenses.

Credit/Debit

Although I may no longer be ahead of the information bubble regarding credit and debit, I'd nevertheless like to spend some time on this topic; perhaps put a new spin on them, for your benefit. Credit and debit are quite different in how they work, yet together they hold an important and interrelated place in our wallets and in our life.

Credit has been a concept used in society probably for as long as recorded history, if not longer. On its face, it seems harmless: the idea that one party extends goods or services to another, based on a mutual agreement that the debt will be repaid, and according to the terms. In olden days, I am sure such pacts were based on both parties being at least somewhat familiar with each other. The irony of credit, though, is that in modern society, credit becomes more practical, yet is abused on an almost incomprehensible level, rendering its potential to do good severely curtailed.

Indeed, one finds it difficult to rent a vehicle, make advance bookings for lodging, make major purchases, etc. without the use of a credit card. Both sides—the consumer and purveyor—have taken the concept of credit, and through misuse and overextension, have turned those credit cards into enemies rather than allies. Don't misunderstand; I am not here at all to judge you, merely to present ways to you in which you can turn credit and debit into allies—very powerful allies at that.

Many major credit cards offer no annual fees for holding the cards, give rewards for purchases, and competitive (though still high) interest rates for payments. Whether we like it or not, the idea of credit and credit cards is so enmeshed in the American way of life that they have become a "necessary evil," and one we have to make peace with. I recommend holding just one credit card, with no higher than a reasonable limit, and only using it when absolutely necessary.

My one credit card is an American Express Platinum business card, which has no fees, and itemizes all purchases for myself and the two others who hold duplicate cards. What is noteworthy about my having been approved for a platinum card, or any card at all, for that matter, is that I've held my American Express card since early 2005—months before my (October 2005) pension commenced. Before my pension, I showed a $5,000 per year income as a crossing guard, and about $3,000 per year from rental income/dividends—totaling approximately $8,000. I know this point will not be lost on you. American Express obviously did their homework on me before approving me for cardholder status; SunTrust, too, when approving me for a $51,000 mortgage on just a crossing guard's wages (June 2004).

Credit *does* speak volumes about an individual, for better or worse. So it pays to take this bull by the horns and wrestle him into submission, lest he gore you. Debit can provide you with the strength and backing to do this. In bookkeeping and accounting terms, to "debit" means simply to subtract from a balance. Debit cards, though generally backed by a major credit card company, are tied to one's checking account. This means that any purchases are immediately withdrawn from the balance of the account. This very element is the key as to how you may now feel safe carrying just one credit card, and how you can avoid overspending. When you are in line at any store and you peer into that checkbook and see before you the balance you have to work with—that's powerful. Staying on a budget below that level, daily, monthly, yearly—for a lifetime— is easy and entirely possible, when you learn to budget by using a debit card for the vast majority of your purchases.

You must begin to think this way: to live within your means. Don't give yourself the buffer zone that credit cards allow, between purchase and month's end. If for some reason you must put something on a credit card, put paying it off in full at the top of your priorities at month's end. The interest on carryover bills is incredibly high when making the "minimum payment." Indeed, you're really not even paying any principal…just paying interest. With the advent of debit, learning to use this tool instead of your credit card will mandate that you live within a budget, while avoiding any interest. The maximum limit depends only on you. I keep about $10,000 in my checking account at any time. The fact that my checking account pays no interest bothers me not one bit. With each purchase, I have paid in full for what I have bought, with the knowledge, too, that my books are balanced.

Debit and credit each represent a good opportunity to establish to yourself and to others that you're living responsibly. Debit cards are accepted almost everywhere nowadays. Even if a certain establishment's machine is not set up for debit purchases, usually they can run the transaction through as credit (remember, debit cards are backed by credit card companies). Beware, however, it is the merchant—not you—who usually gets to decide whether the sale will go through as debit or as credit. So even though your debit card may have the Visa logo on its face, you must be ready for a debit to your account. No shortcuts!

Just decide right here and now that you'll be the best friend to yourself (and to your family) that you can … that you will avoid, from here on out, any type of financial activity which can only add to your burden, or keep you from ever making retirement a reality. Whether through excessive credit card use or by purchasing property or goods beyond your means, you are doing just one thing, and that's ensuring the wrong kind of job security … making certain you will have a job into later life. I know of an officer in my former department who has done just that. He purchased a huge new home, incurring a $2,000-per-month mortgage payment. The home is beautiful, and for now, the officer has been able to keep up with the payments. But the amount of overtime and off-duty jobs he must work in order to make ends meet is troubling.

Believe me, in police work, with its odd hours, stress, danger, and office politics, you will begin to feel the wear on your mind and body relatively early on. Avoid anything which will strain your budget more than necessary. I want to touch on social security, too, since in essence it is a form of credit, credit you will hopefully earn for your years of contribution.

Depending upon which politician is speaking at the time, you'll hear either that social security is viable or that it will fail in the future. Not being an expert on the subject, I can't say for sure whom we should believe. But remember three things about social security, which *are* facts: 1. Social security inherently is a generation behind. In another words, the first group of entitled persons to collect had not paid into the fund, simply because for most of their working lives, it did not exist yet. 2. Americans are living much longer, meaning they are collecting social security longer, which of course drains the fund. Moreover, a record number of "baby boomers" are set to begin retiring. I believe the baby boomer generation (born 1945 to 1959) is the single largest group ever born within a fifteen-year period in America. World War II was finally over, and America was alive with joy and prosperity. 3. Of this, everyone agrees: Social security was never designed to be a sole or even primary source of income. On a dinner plate, social security should be relied on to buy the peas, not the steak and dessert, along with the beverages.

If you plan your retirement responsibly, then whatever you ultimately do collect from social security will be pennies from heaven. It is best, though, to begin collecting your benefits as soon as you can (age sixty-two). Although by waiting, your benefit would increase, you run the risk of waiting too long and never collecting. I applaud President Bush for establishing government savings initiatives. For example, last spring (2006) at tax time, I was told that if I was to set aside a portion of my tax refund into an I.R.A. that Uncle Sam would add to it, as a reward for saving. I did, diverting $1,000 into an I.R.A., and I received an additional $250 from the U.S. government. That is a phenomenal deal, readers ... equating to an instant return of 25 percent on my investment. Plus, this money is tax-deferred.

Kathy, my girlfriend, was of course given the very same offer. For her, though, it was not practical to set aside any of her tax return, for she has recently purchased a first home. New homeowners generally require extra money for renovations, initial deposits, etc. Kathy is still on solid ground, though, even without having been able to take advantage of that particular tax incentive. Home ownership—long the American dream—is of itself an excellent investment which also offers many tax benefits. Take advantage of any incentives you can; add to that an aggressive, long-term savings and investment regimen and a goal of attacking and eliminating debt—and you've got a recipe for accelerated net worth and greater freedom. Avoid playing games with yourself where you just put your debts out of mind; that won't make them go away and only pits you against yourself. Set upon a course of financial self-discipline, making it as fun as possible. It's a great feeling to sit in a home that is all paid for, and enjoy the things you have, all paid for, too.

I know of many people who cannot answer their phone because creditors are calling. My God, imagine how different their life will be if instead, they had credit card companies, banks, Realtors, etc. calling, all clamoring for their business.

Rather than merely closing out this chapter by offering a brief pep talk (as I have done elsewhere in this book), I have put together a list of possible solutions to the burgeoning problem in America regarding debit and credit management, that I think may be useful. Perhaps the right people will come by them, pick them up, and run with them. First a tip for everyone: Use your debit card to either teach or relearn managing your money; and should you have bad credit, practice better buying habits by using only your debit card until you have retrained yourself. Even establish a "debit fund" by setting aside $10 of every $100 you manage to put away … Build your debit fund up to say $500 (or more), then go out and enjoy it. Sure, you could have put the entire $100 away, but rewards are important. Besides, there is no damage done to your net worth, because you would incur no debt if you spend money from a debit (versus credit) account.

Second, if you find that you're feeling depressed, avoid at all costs the impulse to shop. It's only a transitory relief and really is a double-whammy, because you will be adding debts to whatever has caused you to be depressed in the first place. Rather, talk to someone—either a trusted friend, or if need be, a professional. Third, I believe government or consumer advocates ought to establish a compulsive spender hotline. Gamblers, drinkers, drug users, suicidal people, even smokers all have someone they can reach out to. Why not out-of-control spenders?

Along these lines, I believe in the idea of criminalizing (misdemeanor) the act of providing/approving anyone below par financially for a credit card. Handing someone who has no control over their spending a credit card is not much different than opening a bar to an alcoholic. Tobacco companies, too, have been found liable for exploiting people's vulnerabilities. The lure of easy money is something all of us are weakened against, and it's time someone in authority realized this. Before being approved for a credit card, one should be required to either 1) establish a fund as backup or 2) prove beyond a doubt their ability to pay.

Okay, now I've earned the right to give you my little pep talk. Shop wisely, count pennies, and never give up looking for the best bargain, the best investment, and the best cost-cutting strategy. Earlier in this book, I quoted a man of war (Sun-Tsu), and now I wish to quote a man of peace ... John Lennon, who reminds us "There are no problems, only solutions." How refreshing and true. What are you waiting for?   Go subscribe to a newspaper and apply for a debit card!

Investing 101

After searching high and low for either a Barnes & Noble, Books a Million, or any other such intellectual atmosphere in which to write this chapter, I found nothing but a McDonald's. At first this frustrated me, because obviously with my spectacles, satchel and book material, I did not fit in here amongst the teenagers, music and happy meals floating around. Then I realized that although my winding up here was unplanned, it was entirely appropriate for this chapter's creation.

You see, it was thirty years ago that I worked my first-ever job, in the summer of 1976, at a McDonald's in Carteret, New Jersey. What a clear message to me of how things have truly come full circle in my life. In the not-too-distant past, I looked into possibly *purchasing* a franchised McDonald's. This is why I have included "Investing 101" in this book... It's time to see about putting that main course I mentioned in "Credit/Debit" on the dinner table. The placement of this chapter, after "Credit/Debit," too, is meaningful. In revisiting "Credit," I realized that some of the fundamentals of investing had already been covered, so this spot in the book was a good launch point from which to move into investing.

For decades, the investment world remained shrouded in mystery, and thus closed to the vast majority of Americans... a world that only the privileged few walked within. Thanks to the age of information and disclosure, though, doors have been opened to anyone with the desire to enter and learn.

I am of the opinion that not only is becoming a savvy, well-educated investor important to one's overall financial planning, it rates as both *paramount* and *central* for anyone who truly aspires to attain financial success. Cutting costs, buying wisely, setting aside money, etc. is only a beginning, and is rendered essentially useless unless you take the next step, and put that money to work, wisely and aggressively for you.

I'll begin by citing a simple, widely-accepted, rule-of-thumb formula for investing: 100 minus your age equals the percentage of your portfolio that you should be investing in stocks. Example: A thirty-five year old should (theoretically) allocate 65 percent of the money he or she plans to invest, in stocks. The remaining 35 percent, then, should go into less volatile types of investments (such as bonds, CDs, money market funds, etc.). Again, I make mention of the fact that I am not certified as a financial planner nor a stockbroker. I base the justification for my writing this chapter as being twofold: First, it is clear to me that this book would be incomplete without its inclusion, and second, I feel comfortable that it is okay to offer knowledge and information I possess about investing, as long as what I write is accurate, and written in good faith. Over the past fourteen years, the duration (so far) of time that I have been an investor, I did much research in many facets of the investment world. In this chapter I will cover stocks, mutual funds, IRAs and CDs. I'll also delve into the *risk spectrum* and other factors you should consider when choosing how and where to invest.

Stocks, which is essence are corporations that list themselves in one of many financial markets in the U.S. and (oftentimes) abroad, offer their shares for purchase to the general public. Privately owned companies (such as Publix Supermarkets in the Southeastern U.S.) offer stock, but only to employees and their families. Publix is not a "publicly traded" company. For purposes of this lesson, I will limit the focus to publicly traded products.

The Dow 30, at the epicenter of the financial arena, is a group of thirty publicly traded companies which are chosen by the exchange because they (overall) best represent an accurate snapshot/overview of the American economy. Also commonly referred to as the "blue chips," these companies are proven giants in American industriousness, productivity, and integrity. Occasionally, one of the companies listed on the Dow 30 gets replaced, sometimes through no reason other than changing times. For example, fifty years ago technology as we now know it did not yet exist. Yet the Dow Jones industrials have been in existence on Wall Street since the early 1900's. Recently, a technology stock replaced one of the longstanding members of the Dow 30. Generally speaking, blue chips are considered a good choice when searching for stocks to purchase. These companies are financial behemoths and thus are better equipped to absorb any ripples in the economy, besides being well-established as industry leaders. All of the companies listed on the Dow

30 are U.S. household names, which for me lends favor to them, because they are companies I grew up with and I trust.

U.S. stock markets are comprised of the New York Stock Exchange (NYSE), also known as the "big board"; NASDAQ, which is technology-weighted; and the American Stock Exchange (AMEX), which is the smallest of the exchanges. These stock exchanges list, track and chart activity within the companies listed in their exchange. Some of the indexes you will see when exploring the financial sector are the S & P 500 (Standard & Poor's 500), the Russell 2000, the Wilshire 5000, and SPYDER. The number you see associated with an index indicates the number of companies that index tracks; and for investors, this is key in understanding the breadth of any fund which invests/follows a particular index. For example, S & P 500 funds invest only in the 500 companies listed on the S & P 500. Generally considered the most popular of the indexes, the S & P offers *risk spread* and *diversity*, besides being a proven performer, return-wise. So then, remember that some mutual funds are tied to indexes (Index funds), while others are not.

By strict definition, a mutual fund is merely a collection of stocks. Mutual funds are categorized, generally, as follows: domestic, foreign or international. Domestic funds invest solely in U.S. companies; foreign funds are self-explanatory; while international funds choose from a worldwide selection of companies (both U.S. and abroad). Further distinction between the funds is made by categorizing a fund as either small cap, mid cap or large cap. Offhand, I don't know the delineation marks among the three types, but suffice it to say that small-cap funds invest in relatively smaller companies; mid-cap in medium-size companies, and so-forth. At the risk of becoming more complicated, mutual funds are further rated for their risk factor. They are also periodically rated on their performance, by Morningstar, who assigns a rating of one to five stars (five being the best). I have never encountered difficulty locating funds with four and five star ratings from which to choose. Generally, funds are rated as either conservative, moderate, or aggressive—all by design—and will so state in their prospectus. Incidentally, the complexity and legalese which plagued these prospecti in the past has recently (by SEC mandate) been replaced with more understandable language.

Many factors—internal and external—come into play when determining market and individual stock and mutual fund performance, oftentimes in direct contrast to a historically good record. Domestic and foreign events (or lack of) inflation fears; even elections or natural disasters all play a part in shaping what is happening on Wall Street at any given time. This potential for instability is a factor in many potential investors shying away from the stock market. Yet in October 2006, the DOW reached the 12,000 milestone for the first time in history—up from just 1,000 on November 14, 1972; and also rebounding from 9/11, 2001, when it plunged below 9000. America and its economy are incredibly resilient, and given time, the vast majority of losses suffered will be regained. You just have to refrain from panic selling, and attempt to remain focused on the broader influences.

The following article, featured in the *St. Petersburg Times, Business,* section (D) P.1 June 9, 2007 quotes those principles advocated by *Investor's Business Daily* pertaining to stock investing/ownership:

Fast Facts

So, you want to be an investor?

Some principles advocated by Investor's Business Daily:

- Buy only when market indexes are trending up.
- Buy only high quality stocks selling for $15 a share or more.
- Look for stocks with accelerating sales and earnings.
- Look for stocks with increasing institutional ownership.
- Learn how to use charts to determine buy points.
- Don't buy stocks based on dividends or price-earning ratios.
- Don't bottom fish or buy a stock with a falling price.
- Sell a stock if it falls 8% below your cost. No exceptions.

Some of the more conservative types of investments include bonds, IRAs (Roth and regular), CDs, and money markets. Savings bonds, the most popular being "EE" bonds (now known as *Patriot* bonds), can be purchased for half their face value, and come in denominations of $25, $50,

$100, $500 and $1,000. The initial maturity is seventeen years for series EE (Patriot) bonds, with the final maturity at thirty years. At maturity, the bond becomes worth its full face value.

Series "I" (or inflationary) bonds, like Patriot bonds, reach maturity at thirty years, but differ in that the purchase cost is the actual face value of the bond. Series "I" bonds are available in $50, $75, $100, $200, $500, $1,000, $5000 and $10,000 denominations. The interest rate earned is based on the *composite rate*, which consists of *fixed* and *inflationary* elements. Interest is earned monthly, with rate adjustments every six months.

As with EE bonds, "I" bonds are redeemable after one year of purchase; however any bonds redeemed less than five years from purchase date carry a penalty of three month's interest.

Until recently, the U.S. Treasury Dept. offered series HH bonds, which paid interest semi-annually in the form of direct deposit. This series bond is no longer offered; so therefore anyone seeking an income bearing option must consider something other than savings bonds. Despite this change, savings bonds should still hold an integral place within one's portfolio.

Investing in bonds is a sound means of saving: one that teaches delayed gratification and offers a way of showing support to our government.

IRAs, both Roth and traditional, though utilized mainly for tax benefits, also represent a means to accrue money safely for later years. With Roth IRAs, most of the taxes associated with the account are front-loaded. Taxes on traditional IRAs are only paid when the fund is liquidated.

CDs (certificates of deposit) are offered by banks and, like money markets, offer better interest rates than savings accounts. CDs require a committed time period of deposit, which can range anywhere from as little as forty-five days to five years, with many choices in between. Of course, the longer a period you commit to the CD, the higher the interest rate paid. Usually, the minimum investment to open a CD is $500, but depending on the bank, it is sometimes higher. By the way, mutual funds also require generally either $500 or $1000 for an initial deposit, with subsequent contributions of $50 or $100 (minimum), depending on the fund. Since most people are at least somewhat familiar with traditional bank investments, more so than with stocks and mutual funds, I want to place more emphasis on the latter types of investments. By far, stocks are mutual funds pack the most powerful punch.

The best way I've found to put together a good group of ingredients for a personal stock portfolio (besides research into performance, integrity, etc.) is to choose companies you favor in your own life. What brand of clothes do you buy? Target, Sears, Dillards? All of these companies offer their stock for purchase. What type of vehicle do you drive? Ford, Toyota, GM? You guessed it—all for sale. My dream portfolio consists of one stock in each of the following sectors: banking, energy, technology, blue chip, biotech,

Bulletproof

healthcare and perhaps auto or retail. Again, in the spirit of disclosure and example, here is a list of many of the stock and mutual funds I currently or have in the past invested in. I'm not recommending any to you (I am not allowed to do that); merely giving you a small idea of just how many opportunities await you.

> *Stocks-* GE, Bank of America, Dial, PSE&G, Disney, Atmos Energy, Colonial Bank Group, Merck, McDonald's, Ford, United Air, ExxonMobil, Walmart, Intel, Lucent Technologies.
>
> *Mutual Funds-* Franklin Templeton, Janus Funds, Oakmark, Vanguard and Fidelity.

When choosing mutual funds, find out what the operating costs are (less than one percent, if available). Traditionally, of all the mutual funds offered, Vanguard has a reputation of maintaining among the lowest operating costs. Also, whenever possible, opt for *no-load* funds, rather than either *front-end* load or *back-end* load funds. Incidently, the term "load" means a sales charge is associated with the purchase.

When putting together an investment portfolio, you should remember the concept of *diversification*. To diversify, you should choose mixture of both more aggressive and somewhat conservative funds; and regarding individual stocks, select from a variety of sectors (example: one from the blue chips, one technology, one energy, etc.). Also, you must decide what your time frame (or, as the professionals say, your *investment horizon*) is—how long you plan to remain invested. One thing worth mentioning in regard to "long-term" versus "short-term" investments is that less than one year, for tax purposes, is considered a "short-term" investment, and thus is taxed at a higher rate. Generally, *investment horizon* is tied to age (example: a twenty-five-year-old might aspire to keep a stock/fund for twenty years, whereas a seventy-five-year-old is inherently thinking in the shorter term for investments). Just as important as timeframe is one's "risk tolerance", also known as nerve. Believe me, when you've purchased a 1,000 share block of a $30 stock and you see it drop $1 in a day's trading (that's a $1000 paper loss), your attention will be heightened, and so may be your pulse rate…And believe me, this will happen. If you believe in that company, though (and, say, something going on elsewhere totally unrelated to the stock is yet affecting it—and that happens, too), and hold fast; you'll likely see the stock price rebound, and even rise to higher levels. Again, your pulse rate will so reflect, but for a good reason.

That's the nature (and lure) of investing. You must have the fortitude to weather the storms, and always think long-term. Perhaps not when it comes to every stock/mutual fund you own, but rather in market strength and the American economy. In fact, regarding your portfolio, experts have recommended that you evaluate your holdings at each year's end for performance. When the bank stock I spoke of elsewhere in the book reached such an incredible level, I had no hesitation in selling. By the same token, when a different stock I owned showed no sign of life, I sold, took the loss, and wrote off that loss at tax time next spring.

Everyone wins and loses. If you do proper research, remain diversified, and give enough attention to your portfolio's performance; however, you *will* be successful at investing.

"With risk comes reward" they say, and it's true. Choose well, and consult a professional is you have a question. Before actually purchasing a stock or mutual fund, track its activity. Each business day (if it's publicly traded) the gain or loss, and usually the week's performance, will be listed in the business/financial section of your local newspaper. Also, you may want to pick up (or subscribe to) a financial magazine whenever possible. It's important to keep abreast of financial matters if you really want to be a player. Any local bookstore, library or supermarket should stock a variety of such magazines. These magazines are both interesting and informative—anything but dry.

Now it's up to you. Seek a professional, or better yet, become your own trusted advisor. Its time to leave this McDonald's. This chapter is completed, and my work is done.

Scenarios

Scenario #1 - Young, new police recruit/rookie, single. Oh, to have the chance to travel back in time and do it again, the right way. Impossible, except vicariously; which is what offering this book can do. I now come to the prevailing reason for creating this, and that is to right a wrong and fill a much-needed void in your overall training.

When I attended the police academy, nothing in the realm of financial guidance was included in the program. Nor was I offered any such information while in field training. In fact, I do not recall anyone within my department ever addressing financial issues.

My greatest hope is that in these pages I can offer you such guidance, by example, and that what I present will be useful to you throughout your career and beyond. In hindsight, even taking into consideration that I have done well personally, I *absolutely* would have fared much better if someone would have turned my attention to such matters.

Your first step forward begins when you realize that of all the stages in your career and life, the rookie stands to gain the most financially by reading and applying the advice you will be given in this book. You are at the ground level of your earning potential, and hopefully also carrying the lowest levels of debt and responsibility of your life.

Having said that, however, be aware that it is virtually impossible to address each and every possible scenario in life. Rather, what I am attempting to do is to categorize the scenarios based on rough age groups and on each "phase" of your career's timeline.

After first reviewing your debts and income balance sheet and calculating your disposable income, you must establish a workable budget. In the chapter "Getting Started," you can find much more information on this topic. For now, though, you must be allocating every available dollar toward your savings. At work, enroll in a regular 457K account program through your payroll department, and begin to contribute. The monies will be taken directly from your paychecks. I believe the current maximum per annual amount allowed is roughly $15,500, so that equates to roughly $1,291 per month you can set aside for this.

The 457K, which, by the way, is the government employee's equivalent of the commonly known 401K, packs a tremendous punch, in that every penny you contribute comes right off the top of your yearly taxable income.

Be aware, however, that the money you do contribute to a 457K cannot (except in an emergency) be touched until you separate from your agency. Once you do separate, though, you may collect it, either in a lump sum or as a structured payout, regardless of age.

Because of the fact that this money, during your career, is virtually unavailable to you, the amount you elect to allocate must be well thought out. What I did initially was to first build a substantial portfolio in traditional (liquid) investments. Then, about seven years before I retired, I enrolled in the 457K plan.

Since my other investments and endeavors were, for the most part, doing well, I only viewed the 457K money as something extra, not something serious. Of course, for each individual, it may be different, but from a practical standpoint, my suggestion would be to divide your savings fifty-fifty, 457K and liquid accounts.

Being young and just starting out, you will need money available for life's major purchases. Tying up all your money for perhaps twenty years would be unadvisable. It is now that you can become the most creative, turn saving into a game or a challenge, and devising new plans as to how you can accelerate your investing. Some examples would include overtime and raises. Overtime can be a terrible master when you need it, because this means you've gotten in over your head. It can also make a useful servant when used to bolster your saving and investing. As the money you have invested increases and compounds, if you want, from time to time, you can take a little, just to reward yourself. You can also use some of this available cash to buy both those necessities and also the finer things in life. Because you have saved it, your money will be right there waiting for you. You will own what you buy before you exit the store, owing nothing to anyone.

I have bought cars—new cars—with cash, since 1993. I took my mom on an Alaskan cruise in 1998 after selling a bank stock which skyrocketed in value, split, and then rose again. I have paid cash for my last two homes, plus purchased one investment house in cash and a second investment condo with a 60 percent down payment. David has had a custom charter boat built, for which he paid cash; and has no home mortgage.

These are true stories, yet so uncommon they seem incomprehensible to most of the people we share them with. But the biggest message I have for you, reader, is that this stuff is powerful, possible, and it works. Back to scenarios, though. As I have mentioned, you are at step one, salary-wise. Again, each department will differ somewhat; with ours, we received step raises every year for the first five years, then every other year thereafter. Retirees also (besides current employees) receive an annual 1.5 percent C.O.L.A., which helps me these days.

Let us say, for argument's sake, that after seven years on the job, you will earn about 20 to 24 percent more than on your date of hire. Dump every penny of those raises/merit/C.O.L.A.s into savings and investments. Do not forget about overtime, either, your faithful servant. All this money is money you are not yet used to having, so in all likelihood, you will not miss it. Keeping enough of a percentage in liquid accounts will enable you to buy what you need without borrowing.

One of the first and most important purchases you will or should make is your home. If you happen to be currently renting, use the term of your lease to save up a good down payment, and then go looking for a home to buy. Research it, buy carefully, of course; but whatever you do, buy!

With very few exceptions, mortgage payments are almost always lower than rent payments. In my area, 2/2 condos rent for $900-$1,000 per month. A mortgage payment on a modest starter home, at today's historically low interest rates would be roughly half that amount, and you would be building equity at the same time. A rule of thumb regarding mortgage payments is that for every $10,000 borrowed, the monthly payment is $50. When you do buy, when you are able to, pay extra toward the loan principle.

Remember, a 6 percent loan payment on a $50,000 note is much less than a 6 percent loan payment on a $100,000 note. Banks know this, of course, and they are all too eager to offer up many tempting options, equity lines, second mortgages, personal loans, etc.

Upon the purchase of my condo in 1996, I did initially take out a mortgage, with the requirement I keep the loan for a three-year minimum before becoming eligible for payoff. I began planning immediately for the day I would in fact pay off my mortgage. Exactly three years later in April, 1999, I contacted my lender, informing them of my intention to settle the loan.

The bank tried everything in their power to persuade me to keep the mortgage, to the extent that I eventually had to have a friend of mine who is an attorney draft a demand letter, wherein he asked for a payoff figure. Shortly thereafter, I paid off my $30,000 fifteen-year note, saving $16,414 by so doing. Imagine how much the savings would amount to on a $100,000 note or higher. This is very powerful stuff, reader, and not the sort of information banks would like to share.

Just for the record, though, the vast majority of banking professionals are fine people; it's just that I don't want them to earn a living off me, nor you, my reader. So then, if you are still living at home and planning to venture out on your own, you should begin to make preparations to buy as soon as possible. Nowadays, most mortgages have no prepayment penalties.

I want to talk now about your second-largest purchase: your vehicle. So many models out there are sleek and attractive, even sexy, with such gracefulness and power. They have to be, otherwise no one in their right mind would invest in something that costs a bundle, depreciates in value, and rusts and breaks down over the course of time.

Let me, for discussion's sake though, concede that you have come up with a good reason to buy that new car. Fine, go ahead and buy it. Pay cash if you can, or at least save up for a substantial down payment. Then pay it off ASAP and keep it ten years if at all possible. That is the only value in vehicles, longevity. After the loan has been paid off, the car is then working for you. My Mustang was paid for in cash in 1993, brand new. When I finally sold it 10 years, 3 months and 114,000 miles later, engine-wise it was still in good shape. It was just a bit embarrassing pulling into art shows with a band of duct tape around the sunroof, and fading paint. Ten years plus without a car payment, and no mortgage payments since 1999 though, was very easy to live with.

Together, conservatively that would amount to a savings of six hundred a month or more. The money I saved in payments I plunged into savings and investments; done right, you can too.

Scenario # 2: A few years down the road, getting married. Congratulations, and may you have everlasting peace and joy. By now, you hopefully will have been socking away the maximum limit both from your regular pay as well as from what you have earned from raises, overtime, and C.O.L.A.S.

Sit down with your spouse and make very sure you agree on your goals and beliefs. I will assume that since the two of you have chosen to get married, you agree on most things, mainly financial. This, the time before kids come along, (but even afterward) is when you should see about trying to perhaps make do on one salary (assuming both work) while socking away the other. Doing so may not seem like too much fun now, even if you have elected to utilize the larger salary. I realize that, and to be honest, sacrificing is not fun. That is, only until you two are sitting somewhere together five years later, going over your finances, and you glance at the numbers and see you have amassed $100,000 or so. That amount is what you would have in a lousy market, in a conservative account, after just five years of contributing $18,000 per year roughly. Those same dollars invested in aggressive funds, during a bull market, however, the sky is the limit. At that moment, when your spouse sees the result of your efforts, then it will all have been worth it to both of you. Perhaps even try to put away the greater of your two incomes. The results will be even harder to believe.

This idea lends itself to the central point in the book, and that is that whatever you do, however hard you try to save and cut your expenses only serves to help you and can never hurt you. Remember that the money you put away is not lost at all, not forfeited, nor are you being deprived of it. In contrast, it is right there for you; it is growing and will become your best friend and servant. Money cannot buy you love, nor happiness, nor health, for the most part. What it can provide, though, is freedom and greater security in an ever-changing world.

These days, I am there for Kathy and my family. I can travel when I want to, or lock my doors and never have to leave home. Money offers such choices.

One just never knows what lies ahead. Moreover, whatever does lie ahead keeps going up in cost: vehicle repairs, health care, clothing ... the list goes on.

Had I not done the amount of preparation I did, there would have been no hope of ever retiring at twenty years, much less prior to and so young. My pension is supplemented by crossing guard wages, rental income, and dividends on stock.

I digress, though, and ask that you excuse me, but in laying bare my own bones, I hope to show you that we all face the same struggles, really. By socking away income into a tax-sheltered IRA or 457K plan, you are also substantially lowering your taxable income levels, which becomes even more important if you and your spouse earn good salaries. At the same time, however, once in a while, it is okay to reward yourselves. We all have to feel we are working for something: For some purpose beyond the mechanical. Most jobs, especially the better-paying ones, bring demands, responsibilities, and stress to your life. Sure, personal fulfillment and valuable experience are garnered as well, but speaking about police work, this is a profession that exacts a heavy toll. You must be ready, financially, when it comes time to leave. That is what this book is about, to confidently go out of service on your terms.

Scenario # 3: Midway through career, with some of life's setbacks, and added responsibilities. This means you have reached the ten-year mark, and thus your pension benefits are vested. Congratulations! Now, at the very least, you have secured a pension for the rest of your life. A word of sage advice regarding this milestone: If you have been entertaining any serious thoughts of getting out, now is the time to do it, for several reasons. First of all, you must allow enough time in which to build a second career, for a ten-year pension (by itself) will be inadequate to live on. Second, you have reached an important milestone and you're still young. You would have the time to still reach peak earnings elsewhere. If you are considering a move to another agency, as difficult as it is at ten years' seniority to transfer without losing too much in salary, it becomes even more challenging as time passes.

They say burnout in police work happens to everyone, generally at about the seven-year mark. By ten years, this feeling of burnout should have passed. If it has not, perhaps that should tell you something. That ten-year mark could serve as a springboard for you.

If you are still in for the second act, though, then read on! As I have said, the primary directive of this guide is for you to always keep adjusting your budget, with a constant focus on both saving and extreme cost-cutting. I realize this may be especially difficult now, as your family may have grown or you have moved into a larger, more expensive home. That is okay though, because the steps are still the same, and there is no one path to financial security.

No matter where in your career you are this book can help you; however, this book contains no magic, and indeed there are those whose circumstances are such that it may be virtually impossible to retire young and secure. I encourage those of you who do fall into this category not to despair; you can still absolutely improve your situation. Quite possibly you could even turn things around; it just might take longer.

All of you though should begin, at this mid-career point, to work hard at paying down debt and reducing spending levels, with the goal of moving closer to a level of expenditure you will live by during retirement. There is no reason for multiple credit cards or multiple car payments. Begin shopping at discount stores; make dining out a treat. Generally, begin tipping the scales more and more toward greater saving and lighter spending.

If you should suffer a major setback, such as divorce—as both David and I have—I am sorry for that. My goal in this book, though, is not to offer personal advice, but to see that you prevail financially, despite such adversity. Just pick up the pieces and begin to rebuild. Divorce is always crippling; in mine I gave away a new villa and its contents. David parted with an expensive piece of waterfront land in his divorce. We still came back just ten years later and retired.

Adversity can be harnessed into a powerful motivating force, and work is great therapy, too. I lost my dad in late spring, 2001, and I can remember taking every available off-duty job that summer. I worked seven days a week through July and August, and basically did not let up until year's end. Aside from easing my pain, I managed to earn $9,000 extra in those six months. When I grew tired, I slowed back down to just regular duty. I know that my dad would not have wanted me to sit around pining. He always preached "Get the money when you can!" You *will* feel the wear of those added hours of work, but remember, after twenty years you are still young and you will recover.

At my retirement ceremony, after being presented with a plaque and letters, I shook hands with the chief, said a few words—and it was over. Besides that, what I can recall was shaking hands with a friend of mine, a detective (now a lieutenant). He took my hand, looked me in the eyes, and said, "I hate you!" Joking, of course, but I got the point.

It's funny how the act of actually going through with "pulling the pin" remains such a mystery with cops; at least it was in my department. It's something everyone talks about in locker rooms or hallways, in lowered voices, but something yet feared and avoided as long as possible.

Upon hearing the news that David and I were each getting very close to retiring, senior officers and even staff were just flat-out mystified about how we were able to do it. One particular captain—true story—actually wanted to know if we had hit the lottery. Three months after I had left, I got word that a sergeant I was always close to had also made the leap. He had been a police officer since Vietnam (m.p.) and retired from our department in 2003, after more than thirty years of distinguished service. I was very happy for him. He had a wonderful wife, lots of money, and dreams of relocating to the cliffs overlooking the White River in Arkansas with Lynn.

No one I had ever worked for was more deserving than Sergeant Samuel Garrett. He had finally completed a long and distinguished career and was a great friend and leader to countless officers and citizens.

Sergeant Garrett never made it to Arkansas. Less than four months from his retirement date, "Sarge" suffered a massive heart attack while at home. The world is a better place by Sergeant Garrett having been in it. He helped thousands over the course of his sterling career, but never got the chance to enjoy a retirement. As much as I know he loved police work, I know by the gleam in his eye when he spoke about Arkansas, he loved his plans for the future, too.

The national average regarding police mortality is shocking: Most cops last five years or less after retirement. We simply have to improve on that statistic.

Scenario # 4: Nearing retirement eligibility—this is your endgame. Many chess masters will rate this stage as most important of the game. To me, the whole game, all twenty years' worth, counts. Since this is your final juncture, though, I will give this phase great weight. Begin to prepare yourself emotionally and mentally for the change to civilian life. Realize that you are a multifaceted, talented individual who has many other roles in life besides that of police officer. The more you look, and open yourself, the more interests you may find. I had always loved to read, but until the day my wife and I separated, I never had much occasion to cook. Soon after being on my own, I discovered that I loved to cook. To this day, it is one of my life's passions.

When you are a cop, you surround yourself with other cops. That is fine; there is a strong bond in a unique job like police work. With me, this is even more the case, as my whole family is, or was, in law enforcement. I have two brothers who are deputy sheriffs; my mom and dad both worked as crossing guards in their retirement. Even after four years out, I can count on one hand the number of friends outside law enforcement that I have. Personally, these bonds for all of us may last a lifetime, and that is natural.

Still, you have to begin to allow degrees of separation from the authority, power, and regimentation—the identity, if you will, that comes with the job. You may decide to accept a part-time job somewhere, and whatever that my entail, it will certainly be a far cry from responding to life-and-death situations and oftentimes changing the course of people's lives.

Look ahead toward retirement day, and plan for it. Fortunately, in my own experience, I had seen a few of the guys transition well into civilian careers. I remember one officer who started part time in real estate and he soon got so busy, he started slacking on his calls. Well, that *did* land him in the sergeant's office; but soon thereafter, he left to start a successful career as a Realtor. Okay, I have spent extra time hammering at you how to approach this transition mentally, and that is because I believe this to be the key in taking that step.

You could have all the money in the world, but until you are up for it mentally you will continue checking 10-8 until eternity passes, or you do. I can name officers on my department with twenty, even thirty years, just plum terrified of leaving, because the world of police work is all they know. As you near your retirement eligibility date, you must intensify your cost-of-living budget adjustments, to enable yourself to keep things in your life running smoothly in retirement. As far as pensions and supplemental pensions (if your agency has one) go, they say never ever take a lump sum for your pension option. The supplemental pension fund, for me, was an entirely different thing. That was not my "bread and butter" so to speak. Besides, I reinvested every penny, and it has grown for me at levels I could never have expected in the types of investment funds cities generally prefer.

In my case, retirement was hardly an adjustment at all, financially or otherwise. I tend to prefer the simple things in life, the mountains, a good book, an early-morning jog; but don't think you can't have any expensive hobbies. These things are fine, just pay cash or pay it off ASAP, if you must buy on credit. Do not fall behind—ever—especially on a (lesser) retirement income. You must also begin to make your money work for you. You have to "put it out there" I believe, in different types of investments, always remaining diversified.

My own portfolio took a tremendous hit after 9/11, as did everyone's. Anyone who says theirs did not is lying. Aside from the tragic loss of innocent lives, our economy was dealt a crippling blow. Only now are we experiencing a broad comeback; 9/11 aside, the economic world we live in is becoming ever more challenging. Diversification then becomes ever more important. Put your money to work for you, both inside and outside the stock market.

I have enjoyed success in real estate, and also as mentioned earlier, I invest in art and antiques. We must, in police work, come to grips with the fact that our profession rests nowhere near the top of the salary pyramid; we are down somewhere near the foundation. You need to ensure you are doing everything possible to bridge the gap. One of the biggest expenses you will find is that of health care coverage. The same goes for all Americans nowadays. Costs are higher; companies are balking at paying for it. The whole thing is a mess. If you are fortunate enough to either have a spouse you can sign on under or worked for a department that provides health care to retirees, then you are way ahead. My department has no such plan for retirees, but I shopped around and was able to find affordable coverage through a major company. Never, in my opinion, opt for COBRA; the cost is ridiculous and when I asked why, the way it was explained to me was that you are insured with a common "pool" of retirees, representing a broad cross-section of states of health. So the cost, I guess, is based on averages, rather than on one's individual merits.

For the thousands of officers throughout the country with families who need coverage, I wish I had answers or easy solutions. I would hope that our elected officials would finally tackle this monster of an issue, and bring us some relief. Our city has evidently been "exploring" providing health care, which for a twenty-year officer would give him or her $200 per month toward the coverage—a start, but it has yet to be approved. As with anyone, all I can do in this book is to offer advice to you within the areas that lie in our control. Regarding health care, it has been suggested that we do everything we can to lead a healthy, active lifestyle. The government and food industry have each stepped up, in that information on health studies and food product ingredients is more widely available now than ever. In sum: This book is designed to maximize and to strengthen your financial position over the course of your chosen career. It does not guarantee riches. Although you may, in fact, be successful and retire young, remember, you may still have many years ahead. Plan accordingly, so you do not outlast your money.

That being said, however, I still believe we spend far too much time at work and not enough time at play. They say, too, that if you are doing what you love, it is not work at all. Explore those pastimes you enjoy and look into perhaps turning one of them into something you can build on. If it makes money for you, besides making you happy, then let me welcome you to a successful retirement.

Over the Top: Extreme Saving Tips

We have reached a chapter that I hope you find as entertaining to read as I enjoyed writing it. Many of the stories herein, while comical and even outlandish, are at the same time true. You may think of me as out of my mind, but in actuality "crazy like the fox" is probably (I hope) closer to the truth.

Let me begin with the tale of the breakfast burrito caper. In the spring of 2001, David and I were working in District 1 of our city, Clearwater Beach. Although the area as become known nationally as a haven for spring break getaways, the rest of the year, it returns to its charm as a small, sleepy little island where mostly everyone gets to know one another. Oftentimes, officers wind up becoming friendly with the clerks at their favorite convenience stores, which represent a cool, dry oasis filled with a trove of delicacies…For us it was no different. There is a considerable amount of down time in law enforcement, and during such breaks in the action, we would meet at one particular *Kwik-E-Mart*. We had a great sergeant at the time, who knew and accepted that at our stage in our careers, we had slowed down considerably but could still be depended upon when things turned bad. So we had this unspoken agreement with the boss that we didn't bother him and he did not bother us.

Each food item in those convenience stores is labeled with a "must sell by" date. One slow night, after midnight as I recall, David stumbled upon such a label, and it registered with him—and at that moment was the dawn of a golden era in extreme savings. None of the items with an expired date on the package can legally or knowingly be sold; this, however, usually means nothing when assessing the item's fitness for safe consumption. The vast majority of expired labels are from just the night before or at worst, the previous day.

We had neither hesitation nor shame in promptly bringing this useful tidbit of information to the attention of our friends, the store clerks. They agreed with us and opened their shelves and display windows with all the "spoiled spoils" to us. Folks from that shift on, food and snacks were no longer a problem! Now back to the burritos... Seems that they too fell victim to the calendar. When the clerks mentioned they were not selling very well anyhow, that did the trick. Before I knew it, space in my freezer at home was absent. I ate so many breakfast burritos, my taste for this Mexican treat had me considering a move south of the border!

We had so much fun combing the aisles tossing chips, snack cakes, sandwiches, etc. onto the counter for the inevitable write-off, all the while playfully threatening to call the FDA, USDA, EPA... everyone, at the first sign of disagreement. I am certain that should anyone in the brass of our department read this story, they would seethe with anger. Did we violate any department S.O.P.S? Of course. But did anyone get hurt, or lose money because of our follies? No. The merchandise could not be sold and was otherwise dumpster-bound. The clerks got the biggest kick out of us, and actually came to appreciate our saving them the trouble of purging those items from the shelves.

The amount of wasted food all over the country is staggering. I phoned David not too long ago and mentioned I was including the *Kwik-E-Mart* story in my book, and he just burst out laughing. We miss those days now, but treasure the memories.

Moving on, though, I must point out that officially I do not advocate you accept any gratuities. On the serious side, let us take a look at a more orthodox way in which to save: eliminating or seriously restricting and controlling the use of credit cards. I keep just one, but cannot remember when I last used it. I have formed an investment company, and the card is a business platinum card. I have issued cards to my associates, and in my case, it is useful to have them for business-related purchases, the vast majority of which are tax-deductible.

But having said that, the advent of debit cards going mainstream, in my opinion, almost renders charge cards obsolete. One's credit score is, however, tied somewhat to credit card activity. In this respect, possessing one, and establishing a solid history of repayment is of importance. I once mentioned to a mortgage broker how I went for years credit card-free, and she was aghast. Credit cards have become so rooted in American society, however, with the lure of instant gratification and the "buy now, pay later" mindset that her reaction should not have surprised me at all. I checked my credit score not too long after that chat, mostly out of idle curiosity—803—I guess something's gone okay...

I cover this topic in detail, of course, in the chapter dealing with credit vs. debit. One great advantage of debit, though, blends in nicely with extreme savings and that is, when you can see in front of you, in black and white, precisely what you are spending—that is powerful. Also, following the purchase, the spending is over and done with when you exit the store with the item. Clean and final; no high-interest-rate payments, minimum payments—nothing—you are all done, and you have paid for it out of money you really had. Debit is so widely accepted nowadays that it's almost all you need. Kathy and I took a road trip in the summer of 2004 from our home in west central Florida, to southern Missouri, and as so often happens when preparing for a trip, I ran short of time and could not make it to my bank for trip money. We made it all the way to Little Rock, Arkansas before (upon spotting a Colonial Bank by chance) I pulled into the drive-through teller and finally drew out some cash. It is a rarity anymore that plastic does not suffice. Indeed, on most cruise ships, you must use a "sea pass" which is backed by either cash or a credit/debit card. But cash itself is not permitted for onboard purchases. Get yourself a debit card and closely monitor your purchases.

True, in most cases the money you keep in your checking account pays little or no interest, but the tradeoff is worth it when you gain that moment-to-moment control over that same money. Leave enough in to cover the routine purchases in life, and deposit more when needed. Thrift stores: I cannot cover cost-cutting without adding this element. Thrift stores are treasure troves for everything from designer clothes to art to valuable antiques and collectibles. Flea markets, a close cousin, are even better, because generally they are larger and offer much more types of goods and consumables. I make sure to load up on fruits and vegetables whenever I go: They are always very fresh and cheaper than in supermarkets. On one such trip to a thrift store, I found a vintage poster from the off-Broadway play *Barnum* (1980). The play listed a then-little-known actor named Glenn Close; and the poster itself was colorful and in mint condition. I paid one dollar and was told by Jim Kennedy of Kennedy Fine Art that the poster is worth $100 to $150.

In Tampa, Florida, at a huge art and antique fair at the fairgrounds one winter day, an etching that I instantly recognized as a Salvador Dali caught my eye. Not knowing its exact provenance or pedigree, the dealer accepted $150 for it, gladly. A recent appraisal by my good friend in Palm Springs California, Mr. Ed Okil, of the National Institute of Appraisers, put the value of the etching at $2,500. Turns out the piece is a rare, early etching by Dali (*Autumn*, 1928) and is considered important. Treasures found in the most unlikely places, had for a pittance... Extreme saving at its best.

Carrying the idea of scratch-n-dent, or used, into other areas of your home and life, explore such stores when in need of appliance replacements. Locally, there is a wonderful Sears outlet. You would be amazed at how reduced the prices are, for damage that is merely cosmetic and very often not the least bit conspicuous. Some of the marks are so minor, they are comparable to such mishaps that occur during the delivery of the perfect items.

Vehicles are another critical area you simply must address, as this purchase, for most Americans, represents the second-largest investment in one's life at any one time. Buying wisely, or unwisely, can almost make or break someone. Fact—if you purchase each vehicle (any vehicle) new and keep each one in service ten years—over the course of a lifetime, you will have saved a quarter of a million dollars. I know what you are thinking: What about repairs? What about if I take care of it and then sell it? I had to read the article two or three times before it sank in.

Remember, this is not a research paper and I do not recall my source; but I assure you the article was run in either a newspaper or investment guide. And I assure you the information is very true. Vehicles, with extremely rare exceptions, never hold their value. And there is almost no amount of routine repair work and maintenance costs that can come near what car payments will run you. Unless you buy the vehicle with cash, too, you will need to keep full insurance coverage on it as well. 1988 was the year I last made a car payment, and I've a swayed Kathy over to my camp—she has never had a car payment to date. Both our cars are working for us—not the other way around.

Mine was previously owned and loved by a ninety-one-year-old lady, who had purchased it brand new, kept it six years, adding just 24,000 miles to the odometer. Kathy acquired hers from an eighty-one-year-old—same story, eight years old but only 33,000 miles on its odometer. Folks, believe me: Old people are not out laying rubber drag racing. They treat their cars like best friends. When they are in positions to sell, jump at these deals—you cannot go wrong. As with any purchase, buy well, keep it for as long as possible; and whenever you have the choice of whether or not to buy something outright or make payments, always choose the former.

Car insurance: Shop around and you will be surprised at how much you can save. I had been a good customer, having insured with a major insurer for twenty-one years. One day, I called for a quote from a company near my area and ended up shaving $280 a year off my bill, for identical coverage. Over the course of ten or twenty years, it is simple math to figure out what that amounts to. The folks at my longtime insurance office are all very, very nice people. But I do not wreck often at all, I do not consume alcohol, and I'll bet the folks at my new company are nice, too. The only difference I can see, then, is that five years down the road, I will have saved $1,400.

We must buy food, insurance, cable TV; they are basic services we are all stuck paying for—so pay as little as possible. Condominiums and townhomes and villas sometimes include cable service in your maintenance fees. Even if you must pay extra for it, oftentimes the community is offered a much lower rate by the cable company because the complex is buying in bulk, if you will. I discovered this quite by chance when moving from one condo complex to another, just eight miles away. Previously, I paid $33 a month for cable, with a maintenance fee of $145. These are reasonable costs here In Florida; however, in my current condo community, the maintenance fees are $138 with cable TV included at no additional charge. That's about $468 right there in savings, with something as residual as a cable bill.

For years, I rented VHS tapes and DVDs at my local supermarket or video rental store. Then I discovered the same products and services were included in my library membership. Without any charge for rentals, we enjoy our movies, and the library volunteer I spoke with one day advised me that they are always expanding their collection. Folks, it is this small stuff that, when taken cumulatively, will kill you in the pocket. Name brands, designer labels, individually packaged or custom products—anything that represents either status or convenience to the buyer boosts costs significantly. Pay attention to details in your life, in your home. Use ceiling fans, turn off lights, boost the temperature in your home just a degree or two. Conserve wherever you can. I even water down the carbonated sodas

I buy! Keep those unused or unwanted gifts you get. Regifting does not make you a bad person. If you are careful, things can go smoothly for years, without a hitch. You can save hundreds and rid your closets of so much clutter.

If you happen to be on the receiving end, conversely, of an expensive product, say good coffee, learn to stretch it by blending it with some lesser-quality grains. The taste will still come through, and it will last longer. Use coupons for everything you can. Shop during sales; look for giveaways, and when traveling, grab packages that throw in those extras. In everything you do, each day of your life, concentrate on cutting everything to bare bones. It is fun, and becomes addictive and adds up over time.

Develop and cultivate a reputation with others as being a tough, smart, but always fair negotiator and consumer. Once others see that you have done your homework and know what you should be spending for something they will not try to get over on you in the deal. By the same token, if you get a good deal and great service, and you have connected with a quality person, then it is not only acceptable but wise to open your wallet. In these cases, the cash you lay out will certainly pay for itself both immediately and in the long run. In my opinion, one of the greatest teachers ever in the art of business is Mr. Donald Trump. He just does things so well. He has class, brains, and style. Many of my own ways of doing business are directly attributable to the priceless lessons I have absorbed from reading Mr. Trump's works—all of them. You cannot put a price tag on talent, and as busy as he is, this came across as one of his biggest points. Find the best, pay them well, and cultivate long-term relationships with them. You will reap so many benefits, both tangible and intangible.

In America, there is so much out there available to you, just there for the taking. Moreover, there are so many different ways to achieve what you want for your life. One surefire way to succeed, they say, is to pursue that which you love. If you enjoy doing something, then it is not work; and since your heart is in it, you will do it well, without even noticing. And so often, as we see all around us, success translates into dollars.

Many of you have chosen law enforcement as a career for the very same reasons I did: "Always wanted to be a police officer since I was a kid"; the desire to serve others and do well in the world. The police officer has a unique opportunity to do all this and more. In my career, I am credited with saving three people's lives, all on separate occasions, during critical incidents. In one instance, the workers in my mom's bakery once called me a hero for what I had done. I don't think I am, but let me tell you, it's a nice feeling to know I did a good job in this crazy world , when it was my time to serve. I am certain each and every one of you can say the very same. There is just simply no other job in the world like law enforcement. Stay in it as long as your health allows and as long as you are happy.

This book is not designed to pull you away from your chosen career—only to help prepare you to move a bit more easily into the outside world when that time does come. Meanwhile, after your shift or on weekends, pay attention to those often-unnoticed details in your life and in yourself. What hobby or interest is attracting your attention? What can you do to cut costs? Where do your talents lie? Are there any courses or training programs you can take to become more diversified, marketable, and well-rounded as a person?

Speaking of training/education, in Florida, officers are paid bi-weekly for accredited training courses, and for having earned a college degree from an accredited institution. Just for holding a bachelor's degree, I was paid $85 per month by the State of Florida. Moreover, my department has a tuition reimbursement policy, which paid for a portion of the courses. Usually, the only two caveats are that the course be related to law enforcement, and that you achieve a final grade of "C" or better. As far as specialized in-service training courses, again, if they were approved by the state—for every two training courses completed, the officer earned $20 per month. I had four which qualified, so that added $40 (plus the $85) to my salary. The officer benefits monetarily, and his or her department cultivates a more well-rounded professional employee, who is that much better able to serve the public.

As far off as retirement may now seem, you are going to reach a day when you will pick up your radio microphone and check out of service on the air, forever. The question is, will you be ready?

Synergism in Partnership

Within the world of law enforcement, the term *synergism* relates to an enhanced effect of two elements which have been combined; most commonly drugs and alcohol. When combined, the effect is not 1+1 = 2, but rather 1+1 = 3. In the case of harmful ingredients, synergism is best avoided, of course; but for purposes of this lesson, that same formula still applies. In business, as Martha Stewart would say, though, "It's a good thing."

It is my belief that partnering yourself with a like-minded, trustworthy, equally ambitious individual will afford you both the opportunity to create more, on a larger scale, than going it alone. Consider this scenario: You have accumulated, say, $75,000 of liquid savings/ portfolio assets, and you are ready to invest it in something. For argument's sake, let us say an investment condo, priced at $110,000. You put together a solid down payment, favorable with any bank, with a relatively small note ($35,000). Now, let us move forward two years or so. Based on both current and historical trends, and assuming you considered the adage "location, location, location" in real estate buying—that property is easily worth say $170,000 (which represents a $60,000 increase). Now recall that your initial note was $35,000. Perhaps you have even paid that note down to $30,000; this would leave you with a gross profit of $40,000 and a net gain of roughly $30,000 at that selling price, after closing costs, Realtor commissions, etc.

First, let us touch on the fact you paid down your note (as much as you could), while at the same time the property climbed in value. Welcome to the world of leverage. Incidentally, that $60,000 figure I plugged in for appreciation, over a twenty-four-month period, is a conservative number in most areas of the country. Now let's take a look at the power of two versus one. Your partner—be it your significant other, friend, or business partner—also has $75,000 ready to invest and add to your common war chest. Here I must diverge in two directions… With $150,000 now at your (common) disposal, you can acquire two $110,000 units—or, by taking out a note of $70,000, you have proportionately climbed to a $220,000 price level of buying power.

I wish I could have shopped in that elevated price range, because generally, the more a property is worth (or, put differently, the larger the unit you buy), the greater the appreciation will be. I do not know of any bank/lender that is not satisfied, generally, with a solid 20 to 25 percent down payment. Of course, I based this assumption on each of you having the attributes of a desirable borrower: good credit, solid job history, etc. So, moving forward, at this point, your buying power with two is far greater. Let us assume you invest in two units priced at $110,000 each, and after those same two years you sell, with an $80,000 collective profit. Of course, you get your initial $150,000 investment back at sale as well; so your war chest now contains $230,000.

With that amount now at your disposal, you have easily elevated your price range to between $300,000 and $350,000, conservatively.

Two makes the ride a lot more fun and exciting. You can turn it into a savings challenge. Should you decide to open a joint savings or business account, you can set goals and establish timetables. Of course, too, there are the options of an LLC or full corporation. Your lawyer or accountant can provide you with information in these areas. If your partner happens to be a spouse, you might try banking/socking away one salary (for your business) and make due on the other salary for living expenses. If some of what I say here spills over into the realm of another chapter, forgive me; some points lend themselves to more than one argument.

Success brings success, and money brings money ... both are contagious and will draw others, personally and professionally, toward you. True story: I have not as yet formed any corporation or LLC; yet last year (2005), I was contacted by a major credit card company, and offered a platinum business card. Although I emphasized to them I did not have a business, so to speak, they were not in the least bit put off. "Just choose a business name," they said, and they would approve me for the card, with additional cards for my "employees." I suppose you could say that my property manager is an "employee" of mine—so I accepted two credit cards, and "Award Investments" was born. All perfectly legitimate (I guess), and a great example of how a successful lifestyle gets noticed by the right people in the right places. My next step, should my holdings grow, is to look into an LLC or full corporation.

I am tired of being on the sidelines, watching all the reality shows on TV, (specifically real estate) which show plainly just how great the opportunities are out there to grow and earn great profits. All we need to do is find the courage and make the choice to reap that fruit. I am convinced that applying sound logic with solid principles and planning, can lead to nothing but success.

Another story worth mentioning, sadly, involves that of lost opportunity, because of not capitalizing on the potential power of partnership. In my county sat a now-obsolete U.S. Forestry Service fire watchtower, located on what I guess to have been one acre of land. The parcel is situated in the heart of a very desirable area in Clearwater, Florida known as Countryside. The property is next to an upscale mall known as *Westfield Shopping Town*, which was visited in 2002 by Her Royal Highness, The Duchess of York, Sarah Ferguson. The land was level, mostly cleared, with an old and dilapidated ranch-style house on it. Because the surrounding area is now so built-up, the fire tower became obsolete, so the State of Florida listed the property for sale, with incentives to the buyer regarding zoning variances. I immediately recognized this incredible opportunity; but unable to purchase the property alone, I approached David. Unfortunately, though, he showed no interest.

The property sold almost immediately, to a physician investor, who has since built two attractive, multi-office professional buildings, complete with impeccable landscaping. Not long after completion, doctors and dentists and therapists began moving their offices in, and the buildings have since been fully occupied. Someone threw a strike, but it was not me that time, because I did not have a heavy enough bowling ball. Synergism in partnership. Whenever I ride by that property, it serves as a powerful lesson to me.

Find someone; it does not matter if they are of a personal or business nature. The old adage "two heads are better than one" is true. Expenses are halved, profits are enhanced, buying power is essentially doubled, etc. This is not even delving into the myriad of tax benefits, business incentives, and liability shelters afforded by forming a corporation or LLC. This past summer (2006), I took a buying trip to New Orleans, Louisiana, and while at a bank there regarding financing for an investment property I was interested in, the representative suggested I form an LLC in Louisiana and perhaps consider relocating. Although taken by surprise, I was flattered by the bank officer's confidence in me.

Through the years, I have made it a point to read as many biographies as I can of titans in American business and industry ... but to attempt to generalize their stories would dishonor them. Having said that, though, a great testimony to each and every one of them is that they all believed in themselves, and had faith in their business ethos, and in the American dream. Remember, too, that by his own admission, Abraham Lincoln had failed in most of his attempts in life other than becoming president.

Suffice it, then, to summarize this chapter with the advice that you build your financial future consistently on a solid foundation with a strict regimen ... always keeping one eye out for a good opportunity, and the other searching for that ideal partner. Someone who will complement, support, and strengthen you in your mutual quest for financial success. This is "synergism in partnership" at its finest.

Retirement to Pension: A Look Back from 2003 to 2006

When I first wrote this chapter, in December 2004, I was aboard a cruise ship headed for the Bahamas, with my mom. The chapter, along with the rest of the book, then got shoved into my desk drawer. It sat there until a month ago (August 2006), when I vowed to move forward and hopefully get my message across, at long last.

I believe this chapter is very important, because herein I plan to lay out for you honestly and in detail how the financial plan I had laid out for myself and adhered to for ten long years worked out. The story begins on January 6, 2003 at 5:00 pm Eastern Standard Time—at which point I was seated at a blackjack table in Biloxi, Mississippi—precisely the moment I became a private citizen.

The die had already been cast: I served my last tour of duty on December 27, 2002, and until January 6, 2003 was out on vacation, compensatory time, etc. My gear had been turned in the week before, badge and ID included. The relief I felt was astonishing. It was as though the weight of the entire world had been lifted off my shoulders. In the two or so weeks before my retirement became official, while I still was "on the books," my squad responded, separately, to two horrible calls.

The first call was in reference to an emotionally unstable teenaged boy who was acting out. When the officer responded, the youth came charging down a flight of stairs, wielding a large knife, heading straight for the officer. Tragically, the officer, whom I knew well, was forced to apply deadly force during this incident. Then, while the normally peaceful community was still reeling from this nightmarish incident, my squad responded to another mentally ill person call, less than a half mile away—also in the heart of my zone. The subject, who weighed nearly 300 pounds, became combative with the officers, and during the course of the officers trying to subdue him, the man stopped breathing and died at the scene.

The officer in the first incident had to retire on a disability pension due to PTSD, and a female officer who was involved in the physical struggle with the second subject was grievously injured and could never return to active duty—she was forced to retire as well. Both incidents occurred during my normal duty hours, and both would have been my calls, as primary officer. Is this to say I am happy it happened to two of my fellow officers, both of whom I knew well? Of course not. I can only say that for me, beginning in late fall, 2002, I began feeling physically and emotionally that my internal clock in police work was winding down and that it was time I got out. The point is that I *did*, and that in retrospect I can say it was for the best in every possible way.

Whether the experiences others will have in the twilight of their careers will be the same, if you will experience those powerful internal forces or not, I cannot say. However you reach that point, remember that you will. It is my hope in this chapter to reassure you of two things: first, that you should listen to your inner voice and second, that if you have planned well, you will have no problem moving ahead into retirement.

It is important I point out that with my department's retirement plan, an officer begins collecting his or her pension on the twentieth anniversary of employment. Police work, of course, falls under a hazardous-duty assignment category, and therefore, a regular retirement commences after twenty years, with full vesting rights at ten years. Many departments instead offer a "25 at 55" retirement, meaning that an officer must put in twenty-five years of service, and cannot collect his or her entitlement until age fifty-five. This difference in plans is huge—which is why I mentioned the second retirement plan—but not the point I wish to illustrate. I was hired September 30, 1985 at my department. I left the department January 6, 2003, *thirty-two months* before my pension kicked in. Now, let me explain how I managed that, and thus illuminate how incredibly powerful proper planning can be.

To bridge the gap between my last regular paycheck (late January, 2003) and my first pension check (Halloween, 2005) I laid aside $100,000 for myself. At first, that figure may sound like a lot, but remember, that was for everything; bills, food, insurance, travel, emergencies—everything in life that could have come along, and usually does. Remember, too, that I had no spouse; no roommate, no one to share life's expenses or to rely on for a second, backup income. I say this not to detract from my wonderful girlfriend or mom—both of whom could not have been happier for me. I say this, rather, to emphasize the confidence I had in my plan, and in myself. Had I ever needed it, both those lovely women would have done anything for me. Between 1993 and 2003, I had saved and invested roughly between 45 and 55 percent of my net income. That amounted to between twelve and twenty-five thousand dollars yearly; a few years it was less, many, it was that much or more. I had structured the timeframe until my pension began, based on several factors. The rough yearly allowance I set for myself was $30,000. Between the fact that I had always, by nature, lived modestly and had relatively few bills by plan, I was easily able to live within that budget. In fact, at the end of both 2003 and 2004, I had budget surpluses; so with each year's passing, it became actually easier rather than tighter to make it to pension.

I did nothing for seven months after retiring—and that was long enough to realize that "nothing" was not for me. I went stir crazy, but did need to decompress from police work. By the summer of 2003, I began realizing a part-time job could do the trick: it would get me out of the house and give me something extra for spending. As it turns out, the job of crossing guard had openings, so I started at the end of August 2003. It was a great move for me—the seventeen-plus years I had worked for my department, I had not been contributing to Social Security/Medicare. Not by choice, but rather because my department had its own "supplemental" pension plan. Although the plan was very lucrative, the gap in Social Security contributions was not a good thing. You have to make "40 Quarters" with Social Security in order to collect later in life; it would solidify my standing if I resumed contributions. Crossing guards here in Florida contribute to the Social Security fund, and so I hit pay dirt on two fronts! I had found a little part-time job I love, while helping my financial future. It's fall 2006 at this chapter's completion and I still work as a crossing guard.

I did a lot of stock trading in 2003 and 2004, and that was a lot of fun. Without even really trying, I made a net profit of $8,600 those sixteen or so months that I traded. I established, through diligent tracking, the "trading range" of two or three blue chip companies. This is almost a science, and as long as you choose great companies, you can trade confidently based on the stock price within this range. I do not want to name the companies, nor dwell on this point longer than to say you can make money on the side in many ways. Stock trading is one of them. I became so successful at trading that to minimize the paperwork which stock trading brings, I got to a point where unless I would net a minimum of $700 on a singe trade, it wasn't worth the trouble. Meanwhile, I was thankful to have the opportunity to spend much more time with my mom, Barbara, and my girlfriend, Kathy. The three of us, when possible, and with each, separately I took many small trips to our favorite places: St. Augustine, Florida; the Gulf Coast casinos etc.

In the fall of 2003, I sold my beloved Mustang, which put enough money in my pocket to pay for a trip to North Carolina with Kathy. Remember how I spoke of winning each battle, each day? By now, nearly a year had passed since my last real paycheck. My only actual income at the time was a biweekly salary of $219 as crossing guard. I had shopped around for affordable health insurance, instead of going with COBRA, and by doing so had trimmed about $300 per month off what would have been the cost. I had no mortgage, no car payment, and was soon to move to a different (nicer) condo and eliminate a $32-per-month cable bill. About that move, I had paid off my mortgage at my condo at "St. Tropez" and had invested about $25,000 in upgrades and remodeling. The condo was only about 840 square feet, so the $25,000 went a long way, and when it sold (in six days), my sale set the record for price within the community, but not before a bidding war had erupted between two potential buyers. My return was $50,000 on my $25,000 in upgrades. I remember telling my dad, who was very old-fashioned, about my plans for the condo: granite countertops, new custom cabinets, wood floors, etc., and him telling me I was crazy. He said I would never get my money back, I guess he was right; I got twice the investment back. My dad was right about a whole lot, but when it came to real-estate, things where changing. They say that since 9/11, Americans have come to have a far deeper love for and attention to the meaning of home. Perhaps that has come to translate to improving one's home as well; who can say?

I have always believed in the merits of real-estate, so I always knew there would be a time I would lean more toward such investments. June 25, 2004; recall now that seventeen months have gone by since retirement, with sixteen months still to go for my first welcome pension check. The property looked so good, I did not even blink when signing. I bought a 1/1 condo in a community called " Audubon Condos at Feather Sound," located in a very upscale, booming hamlet in southern Pinellas County, Florida. The developer assured me the asking price of $109,900 was a great deal, and that the unit was sure to appreciate in value. The community was in a prime location, with my unit boasting views of a lake and golf course. That Realtor really called it—recently, in the summer of 2006, I saw an identical unit for sale in the Audubon Community for $179,900, with no upgrades. That price amounts to an appreciation in value of $70,000 ... $70,000 just for simply holding on to a unit for two short years.

The unit has been rented out almost since the day I purchased it, and this October (2006), it will fetch $900 per month. The property has generated a positive monthly income for me all along, and provides a strong tax incentive as well. If you do purchase an investment unit, be sure to have it managed by a rental agency. Century 21, I know, does property management, and although I have found satisfaction with this company, there are many others from which to choose. It only matters that you go to a professional in the field. Your experience as a landlord will be worry-free, even if things turn bad with the tenant. The property management company handles everything, typically, with a fee of first month's rent and 10 percent thereafter. Believe me, it's well worth the cost: at $900 per month rent, that amounts to a whopping $90 per month, or $1980 yearly, all tax deductible as a business expense. Once you develop a working relationship with your property manager, and come to trust him or her, you can even make all arrangements, wherein you do not even have to be disturbed for minor blips that may occur.

In my case, I applied for an American Express business charge card (that one credit card I spoke of) and had a card issued to my property manager at Century 21/Sunshine Realty in Clearwater, Florida. Any purchases made are listed separately on the bill, which serves perfectly as a record for tax purposes. When investing in any property, it behooves you to put down as much as humanly possible, percentage-wise, at closing. Aside from avoiding P.M.I. on the mortgage payments, it just may mean the difference between the numbers working and not working. Let me explain. In my deal, I put $60,000 down at closing (about 55 percent), which left about a $51,000 mortgage note. A simple formula for calculating principal and interest payments on mortgage notes is this: $50 in payments for every $10,000 borrowed. If you ask any banker whether this is accurate, they will probably leap up from their seat and shout all kinds of things at you, such as "that's depending on interest rates" or "type of loan," etc.—and they will be correct.

But I did not make up that formula; all I can say is it does come somewhat close, and is useful in a pinch. So, for a $51,000 loan, that would mean roughly a $260 per month payment. Close—mine was $282. Since then, my rate—an "ARM"—has readjusted, boosting the payment, of course. But it is still very much worth it for me to have kept ownership of the unit and, I can always refinance the loan. The extra $230 more in monthly payments now is offset by the unit climbing approximately $3,000 a month in value. Wouldn't you agree? Along with the mortgage payment comes a monthly maintenance fee (for common-type dwellings: villas, condos, town homes). These maintenance fees do vary, but generally range from $100 to 200 per month, depending on the amenities and the size of the unit. The fee for my unit is $183 per month. Taxes are another factor to consider—mine are $200 per month, which is quite high. When the Zip Code is seen as being a wealthy one, you pay. But remember, at tax time, many of these expenses are deductible. So $282 + 200 +183 out of 85 (fee for $850 of rent at the time) totals $750 a month expenses. That means I was clearing $100 per month, right away, on a unit going up considerably in value.

If the numbers work, make the deal. This fall (2006), I plan to purchase my second investment condo, this time near Ashville, North Carolina. The 1/1s are priced at about $120,000 with a maintenance fee of around $100 per month, but boast drastically lower taxes and insurance costs. Since the catastrophic hurricane season of 2005, Florida has been in a tailspin over insurance coverage.

Back to the North Carolina deal, though, let's run the numbers. I plan to put down approximately $30,000 on a $120,000 unit, which equates to 25 percent. Solid, and I avoid that P.M.I. So, a 90K note, which equals about $450 in mortgage payments, plus let's say $250 total for taxes and maintenance. For North Carolina, that should come in close. The total payments are, then, about $700. I already know that rent in that area for my size unit ranges from $725 to 775 per month, I assume, depending on the view. Even with such a modest profit margin, that deal works. If you buy in a good area, the property will appreciate in value; the tenant will be paying your mortgage, and the taxes incentives are there, too.

This particular condo complex is just over a year old, so they should stay nice for some time. As long as tenants are selected carefully, you should avoid any significant damage or excess wear and tear on the property. With Audubon going smoothly, and Kathy due for a vacation, we took a long trip in August 2004 to Missouri and Arkansas. And that November, still doing fine on my pilot plan, I bought my first Rolex watch, an 18-karat Oyster Perpetual that still adorns my wrist today. Rarely do I ever buy based on a name or brand, but after eleven years of preparing, I felt it was time to break the rules and indulge myself. While on vacation in Arkansas, I also got news of my land in Hayesville, North

Carolina (I owned two acres, which I had purchased for $9,000 late in 1997) selling at two and a half times the purchase price. Practicing delayed gratification, I took not one penny from the $20,000 net figure. Rather, I paid my mortgage note down by $10,000 and sunk the rest into a complete kitchen remodel where I live, in "Pine Ridge." When you pay down a mortgage note in any significant amount, you can have the bank or mortgage company re-amortize your payment amount.

Of course, banks being banks, they charge you for this service—usually in the range of $250. In any case, shortly after I paid my note down, the loan was about to readjust, as far as the interest rate. Because of this, the bank was forced to do the re-amortization without charge. So, do you see how things begin to work for you when you set upon this type of course? By January 2005, with two years having passed successfully and my pension closing in that coming October, I began to feel strongly about my plan's ability to come through. It was at about this time that I began to work more on this book. All the seeds I had planted had finally begun to sprout. My land in North Carolina was beautiful, and I had always planned to hold on to it, and build. Quite by chance, the association there voted to successively raise minimum square footage requirements for anyone who wished to build. My idea was to have a modest but beautiful twin-peak chalet built—but at about 900 or so square feet, it was considered too small for their tastes. When I learned how much the land had appreciated in value, all my disappointment at being turned down in my building idea melted away, and I cashed in, putting the money to great use elsewhere. North Carolina has an abundance of land, and when and if the time comes to buy more, I will have much more money going up there with me. It's the same story for Audubon: Given that it appreciates $70,000, give or take, that means I will have $140,000 in my war chest instead of $60,000. Meanwhile, my condo at Pine Ridge has appreciated nearly $100,000 in two years, as well. Believe me when you start adding figures like $100,000 and $70,000 and $45,000 and $15,000 and more as time passes, and you keep making those deals, it adds up to a very nice sum. Moreover, the longer you forestall actually pocketing any of the proceeds, the larger the amount you have when you do finally cash out!

The tax laws provide for 10-31 transactions when reinvesting in *like-kind* property, which packs a great financial benefit to the savvy investor. How it works is like this; You own an investment condo that you bought for, say, $100,000. You decide to sell, for let us say $150,000. That is a profit of $50,000, which normally is taxable as a capital gain. But, if you take that $50,000 and reinvest it into a similar type property such as another condo, or land or a house, then you defer paying any taxes, as long as you continue to reinvest your gains. You cannot take the profits and use them to buy other types of property (such as a car or art); it has to be reinvested in something similar. It does not have to be exact, though, nor does the purchase have to be in the same state, since this is a federal tax law. Any licensed Realtor should be able to point you to a qualified 10-31 agent. I have not yet had the opportunity to utilize this great provision, but I plan to at first chance.

One of the people I most admire is Mr. Donald Trump. I am an avid follower of his, and have read and reread all of his books. His latest, *Think Like a Billionaire*, was especially meaningful to me, though. In it, he tells all of us to aspire to be a billionaire and to dare to set our sights high. Yet being so down-to-earth, at the same time, he speaks of how he price shops for toothpaste! I highly recommend all of his books, but one other point well taken in *Billionaire* is to surround yourself with the best, and empower them with trust and authority. I found Ms. Teresa Blakesley, and after some time, I learned to relax with things and let Teresa run them; and because I have chosen well, she has never let me down. Set about getting started, reader, because we all have only a certain number of days in which to make hay.

Social Security was never designed to be someone's bread and butter; and with rising costs everywhere, companies are curtailing the practice of providing pensions or health insurance. All of us must endeavor not to outlast our money, but instead prepare wisely and live reasonably; because there probably is a tomorrow. Tighten your belt, accumulate as much as you can, and put your money to work for you in different arenas. Another essential quality you must strive to cultivate in yourself is *adaptability*. Should something you do try flop, you must be diversified enough to bounce back, and have other interests on which to fall back. I have been an avid art collector since a cruise to Alaska in 1998, and I have amassed a fairly large collection for a private individual. My dream has always been to open a quaint little art gallery where I can discuss art and maybe get a return on my investment. To that end, hearing about the "wonders" of the Internet, I enlisted the help of a talented friend of mine, who built me a nice Web site. I figured until I find that perfect location for my gallery, I could at least break into art dealing via my site. I was wrong, very wrong. The endeavor was an utter failure, something which I was not used to.

Art is a very different product than G.I. Joes or knickknacks. Viewers are not going to look at some photos of your $10,000 work of art and write a check to someone who is maybe hundreds or thousands of miles away. At first, it really bothered me that I could not sell a single work of art; after all, *I* had bought it; the provenance on the art was bona fide, and I was sure the pieces were priced appropriately. Fortunately, I came to realize that in the sales world several factors—many of which are beyond the control of the person selling—are in play. When the economy is tough, and folks are concerned about such things as gas prices or hotel rates—in general everyday expenses—they are not going to plunk down thousands on a rare Picasso print. These people are going to hold on to every penny. Eventually, I made peace with my art, and now I am just enjoying my collection and still dreaming of that gallery someday.

The main point, though, is to never put "all your eggs in one basket." I remember joking that my art collection, although valued for insurance purposes at over $100,000, could not at any given moment buy me a candy bar. Fortunately, I had irons in many other fires that could. I recommend you ensure that you do, too. Whatever you do invest in, big or small, do it the old-fashioned way. By this I mean, in my opinion, never (other than an emergency) tap into your home's equity, nor extend yourself in any way. As I have said, the one credit card I keep has a zero balance, always. It does not matter how smart or talented you may be; building too much, too fast can spell ruin. A very good friend of mine In New Jersey went bankrupt when he chose to build on others' money, and on loans and credit, instead of on his own foundation. He paid for his cavalier ways for years. Recently, he has gone into business again. Only time will tell if he has learned his lesson.

I truly believe there are no shortcuts. It is okay to want all you can get; just go about things honestly, and hurt no one in the process. In the summer of 2005, just before my pension commenced, Kathy and I took a long vacation to New Jersey, where I am from. Everything had gone as planned financially and I celebrated the first paycheck's arrival (October 31, 2005) with a memorable dinner with Kathy, David and my mom. Those three years from 2003 to 2006 were a gift, because money buys you just one thing: freedom. As it turned out, those three years would be the last ones I would spend with my mom, which in retrospect only makes me appreciate the time I got to spend with her more.

My mom passed away on April 1, 2006. And had I not retired when I did, who knows how much we would have missed? Police work is one of the most demanding, stress-filled professions known. The best decision of my life was to get out when I did. Stress is now thought to be even more debilitating than originally believed. In the four-plus years I have been retired (knock wood), I have had just one stomach virus, not related in any way to stress. The virus was going around at the school I crossed for, and I am quite sure I was somehow exposed to it. In closing, I wish to say that money definitely does not buy you happiness. The best years of my life were my college years—running around with my friends, playing soccer, working part time, for a mere fraction of what I earned in my career. Yet I had not a care in the world.

Sometimes I cringe at what I had to go through to get back to those carefree days; but the point to you, reader, is that all of you must go through it, too. What I want to reassure you all of is that I did get there, and young, and I believe you can too. Take what you can from this book, add what you can, but start now and start wholly.

Bringing It All Together: Essential Points

The advantage of an average, college-educated street cop who completed a career in law enforcement authoring a financial guide is that by nature, the material I wish to get across to you has been laid out in practical, understandable terms. That, at least, is my hope. From the onset, I decided this book was absolutely not going to be related in any way to either a research paper or any scientific document. No, this is a readable, firsthand account of how two cops, just like you, got ahead financially and got out on our terms. This book is, for me, the culmination of an effort to bring together hundreds of bits of knowledge, gained through the course of a career in law enforcement, a formal education, and most importantly, a thirst for knowledge that has driven me to learn how to get ahead financially—on a cop's salary. Now my wish is to help you get where I have, by exploring and testing the ideas herein.

To my knowledge, no such guide exists which addresses *financial* training for you, the law enforcement community, on what I believe is an utterly crucial topic. What I preach will not help you survive in a gunfight, nor help you win in court, but will bulletproof you in the financial world, outside of your duty hours. Shortly, I will get to the "bullet" points of this chapter, but first you have this one final assignment, and that is, for the rest of your life, go on that very same fact-finding quest that I have.

In the movie *Wall Street*, one of my favorites, the character Gordon Gekko notes that the most valuable commodity he knows of is information. It takes but little consideration to see why ... To the warrior, knowing an enemy's size, strength, and habits can ensure the probability of victory. To the police officer going to a call, the more background information about the suspect and situation, the better, often making the difference between safety and peril. To sailors, accurate charts, weather conditions, and knowledge and seamanship are all-important.

So, each day, set aside some quiet time to study the newspaper (every section). Flip to your locally available financial broadcast on TV. (I like the *Nightly Business Report* with Paul Kangas, among others.) It is understandable, and entertaining as well. It runs just thirty minutes, but it is time well spent; but make sure you don't turn the dial until after the famous "best of good byes" is bode by Mr. Kangas. Another favorite of mine is *Mad Money*, hosted by Jim Cramer. More than once, I have bought a stock which was featured on these programs, and made money doing so.

In the Saturday edition of my local newspaper, the *St. Petersburg Times*, they feature several real estate sections, which highlight local and distant properties of many types. Nowadays, Saturday mornings are my work time—on my sofa in bedroom slippers, sipping strong coffee, listening to

Bulletproof

Bob Marley or Esteban, scanning carefully for those hidden gems in my chosen mine. "Audubon" at Feather Sound was one such find. At last inquiry, my unit there had appreciated $70,000 in two years since purchase.

I have also purchased property on Cape Cod, Massachusetts, Missouri, Texas, and North Carolina—all found within the real estate section of the *Times*. The $100 a year I pay for a seven-day-a-week subscription has made me a fortune. And that is just in real estate.... There are wonderful buys on antiques, art, jewelry, etc., all of which, if bought wisely, and only as part of your overall holdings, could spell a great investment. This is the first of those essential points: Begin planting seeds in a variety of sections of your financial garden, if you will. Cash/liquid savings must take precedence, though; remember, you *do* need money to make money, generally; at least in the beginning. The condo at Audubon I mentioned, I had to save and put down $60,000 upon purchase in order to acquire the property. Banks are generally nervous regarding their investments; and my personal lender told me honestly that my substantial down payment sealed the deal. Everything that flows has to begin somewhere. This is the hardest part—getting started, and following up with patience and fortitude. After that, as time goes on, the water levels of your savings will rise.

It is then that you will see that your money will by itself inherently begin to generate more money. That $70,000 rise in property value took nothing on my part to happen. I am planning to upgrade the unit with granite in the kitchen and bath, but as yet have not. Such upgrades only enhance property appreciation. With my experience of financial success, I found that I actually had to re-adapt to a new lifestyle of newfound prosperity. Please believe me when I say this not to brag, but rather to highlight how stark the change was. Indeed, it took me by surprise. Overnight, for example, I just said to Kathy, "Heck, let's go out to eat"; something that had never really been commonplace without an occasion. The following few days, I then found myself making some impulse purchases at the mall. In short, I realized I was violating the very rules I set and lived by for the past thirteen years! What struck me, though, which is the point, was that I had made no dent in my security or bottom line whatsoever. Do you see what I mean?

Adapting to my success was at first a strange feeling too, and believe me, I am still learning how. Old habits, as they say, do die hard. But prepare yourselves nonetheless, because that is what does await you for your effort, and it is great. Will I ever abandon all those great but everyday habits/values I preach? Of course not. A funny story: One Sunday, my mom and I stopped for takeout at a nice Chinese restaurant near where she lived, and I found my self grabbing extra condiments! Every bit counts, no matter how small it may seem. Each and every day, if you win the battle, you must then win the war. Gather as much information as you possibly can. Remember my motto: "Live like a monk, save like a madman." Make this your credo as well. Put your money exactly where it will do the most for you; but remember, you first have to save and accrue enough capital in order to make entry-level investments. Although I want you to get started right away, know that the impact you feel in your life may not be evident at first.

Recall the story of how I'd squirrel away money with my mom until each time I had reached one or two thousand dollars. After I had reached those amounts nine or so times, and thus started my first "portfolio" of stocks and mutual funds, I would "feed" each one, watching them grow. When I made a deposit, that fund would go to the bottom of the pile until all the others had been added to. Keep *three*, *six*, or *nine* in your mind when considering the number of stocks and mutual funds you maintain; as experts say one should never have less nor greater numbers in a personal portfolio. One day, not too long afterward, I looked at my portfolio and found I had made a great start. The rest, as they say, is history. The same goes for David, as it can for you. Come to understand the financial world forward and backward and inside and out, and learn how to walk within its circles. Become your own financial broker, student, and planner, finding out all you can on your own. Go to a professional when you feel you must, but pay for services only when necessary, price shopping all the time. Watch every penny as if it is your last, and spend wisely. Learn to cook well. It will save you thousands of dollars over the years; you will impress the heck out of your wife, girlfriend, or guests. And on those special occasions in life when eating out is truly called for, you will enjoy the novelty of the experience all the more.

It is at once both sardonically funny and troubling that how it is those very things essential to all of us that hit us hardest in the pocket: insurance, food, transportation, energy, and entertainment, to name just a few. These are closed shops, reader, and we must all pay our dues. And we are not the ones making the rules ... So I say just make very sure you secure the best bargains on everything you must have, and use as little as possible, all the while socking away as much as you possibly can. Play financial games with yourself. One such game I play is with my power bill. On each month's bill, beginning after one year at your current address, there is a box that gives me a comparison of the same month's bill last year. The statement gives you your energy use in kilowatts, then and now. I try every month to beat last year's figures. Sometimes I do, often it is a tie, but it keeps me on my toes, thinking about things like, do I need that air this low, or that light on when no one is in the room? For years, David and I carpooled to work, and these days, it is to Super Wal-Mart, to do our shopping, mostly food. We each buy what we must with (as always) an eye for bargains, and try to spend less than the other at the register. The loser pays a two-dollar penalty to the pot, which then goes to buy two Power Bars for us, which serve as lunch.

Believe me, you cannot imagine the scene at the register, two grown men acting outlandishly in a "who is the greater miser" contest. People just stare, but we have a ball, all the while saving God knows how much money along the way over the years. We share information on bargains in food, gasoline, insurance, maintenance fees, clothes, etc. ... the list goes on and on. I thought I had David beat one day, in the footwear department, when I proudly announced I had located a pair of $4.88 "shore mates." Well, to my surprise, David showed off a $2.87 pair of athletic sandals he had located. Even so, not bad right? Two shod men for a grand total of $7.75! Remember, as they say "The devil is in the details."

Recognize and use *time* as one of your greatest allies. Compounded interest, reinvested dividends and profits, great saving habits, and extreme frugality over the course of time, all will bring along that snowball effect you have all heard of. Delay your gratification in every aspect of your life. When you sell something or something matures, take none of the proceeds. Dump them right back into the pot, and just keep doing so until the pot is full. Then, fill a dozen more pots. Listen to the sages, and listen to none of the sexy, exciting ads you're bombarded with on the television, in the newspapers, on the billboards. Instead, read and delve into the articles in the very same newspaper until you discover those gems that are always there; those things that can make you money, not part you from it.

I believe it was Shakespeare who had said 'Avoid borrowing and avoid lending, each as if they represent the plague.' If you must borrow, generally speaking, that means you cannot afford it, and the same goes for lending to another: nor can they. I offer gifts these days, never loans. I make a decision as to whether they are going to get the money, and ask them not to speak of repaying me; just take it, I say, and use it wisely. And when their circumstances improve, I tell them to put some aside for that next little surprise that awaits all of us. Buy wisely and take care of your property, and get as much mileage out of everything as you can. I once lost the soles of a pair of running shoes during a morning run, right out there on Countryside Boulevard, in Clearwater, Florida. I got home, still wearing the shoes, and later, when my girlfriend Kathy happened to pick them up and noticed they lacked soles, let me tell you, she was in utter disbelief.

So, too, was my plumber, when he noticed all of the pipes to mywater heater were dried out and rusted, at a service call. Smiling and looking up at me, he asked rhetorically, "Your water heater didn't just die, did it?" Knowing there was no use trying to baloney him, I admitted sheepishly that the water heater had died nine months earlier—that prior fall—and that I had actually made it through winter without any hot water. Those stories go on and on.... En route back once from North Carolina, just outside Atlanta, another of my extreme savings practices came back to nest. I finally lost the tread on one of my tires (that was probably twenty-five to fifty thousand miles over its projected lifespan); but when the tire dealer attempted to sell me a replacement, I tried in earnest to convince my mom it would be okay to limp home to Florida on a doughnut. My cajoling did not work with her, but I tried! Anything to save a buck. I drove the Mustang until there were no brakes left, no paint left etc.

When I finally did bring it in for a brake job, the mechanic said he had never seen anything like the condition mine were in. He said I actually had no brakes left...

Please know I am not advocating that anyone ever jeopardize their health and safety. In my own zest to save, I realized in retrospect that I had gone inadvertently too far, when the condition of these things was pointed out to me. A mechanic I am not; I just buy the cars cheap, hold on to them for a long time, and forestall whatever expenses I can. It is amazing how little, comparatively speaking, we really need in order to enjoy life, at least me: a good book, a walk on a quiet beach, a sunrise or sunset, time with that special someone all cost nothing and yet are priceless. I believe, too, that it is infinitely more important to eliminate or at least cut debt/expenses than to earn some tremendous salary and live "La Vida Loca." Stated simply, "it's not what you earn, but what you keep." My goodness, you hear about it all the time of professional athletes, movie stars, heirs and heiresses, entertainers, etc., all of whom earn fortunes only to lose it, ending up living out their days in debt and even poverty. Sure, this is an extreme example of what happens to a popular few, but sadly this does occur on every level. You don't need to make a fortune in order to attain financial security.

You must remember that, for example, if you have saved $15,000 but are carrying credit card debt of $10,000 (which, by the way, is now the average in the U.S.), then in actuality, all you have is $5,000. You have to learn to see things this way. Free yourself from debt first, and then begin to focus your attention on savings. When you have amassed enough raw cash, then begin to invest, as I outlined earlier. For me, such investing has been in stock/mutual funds, art, currency speculation, real estate, and antiques/collectibles. This is so far, at this book's writing: I am always open to new investment opportunities. You just simply have to be. I can tell you too, in the same breath though, that it is virtually impossible to throw a strike every time. It is also fair to say that at least one, if not more, of your attempts will pay off, sometimes, sooner or later.

While sitting in a nice hotel lobby in Hardy, Arkansas in August 2004, I got a phone call from out of the blue, regarding land I own in North Carolina. I had been trying to sell my land for about two years, off and on, since learning the association there had raised the minimum square footage for dwellings to what would be tantamount to a small mansion. Well, my Realtor gave me welcome news that my land was under contract at full asking price—two and a half times what I had paid for it; but that is not the point ... Remember *delayed gratification*. To this day, I have yet to see a penny of that money. The entire sale price went toward paying down the note at the Audubon condo; the other half turned my dull kitchen at home into a gleaming/modern HGTV-caliber showpiece. I did not even keep enough leftover cash to eat at a McDonald's. Theoretically, it could be years before the cash ends up in my pocket, but I can guarantee you that when it eventually does, it will have grown to an even greater amount. Sculpt your net worth just as Arnold Schwarzenegger did his body and his stellar career. Feed it, care for it, respect it, and watch it closely, as you would anything important to you. Never, ever give up, and always thirst for knowledge and for wealth.

The hallmark of the wealthy is to never have enough, to remain driven to have more. Some say that this is the curse of the wealthy. I will cover more on what I hope to do in the coming years, and years ahead in the epilogue, "A Look Forward," so for now let me just offer that you should never stop looking toward the horizon for that next great opportunity. Do not worry—you will know it when you see it. Just take the time to investigate things, without undue hesitation, and then if it seems right, go for it enthusiastically. For now, though, it's time to lay the foundation. Build on a strong base, backing yourself as you grow, with your own capital; always the old-fashioned way. Clever, catchy, quick-buck schemes are never preferable to hard work and perseverance. News abounds of both individuals and corporations that failed to heed this sage advice, at their peril. One more story too, about failure—mine—in my endeavor to pursue art dealing as a viable business. For two years, remember I had a Web site, offering some of my best pieces in a beautiful collection, for sale. In those two years, I sold not one work online. I had given up and discovered my second love: real estate. Then in 2005, I received a peculiar phone call from my brother Brian, regarding one of my pieces of art. Out of the blue, it seemed an attorney from

Chicago had seen the work (still posted on an inactive Web site) and wished to purchase it.

So here I am, wondering why I could not sell a single thing when I was really trying, only to make a sale on a piece not even for sale any longer—two years later! Go figure. You never, ever know when something will hit. Actually, two other pieces sold soon thereafter, but not through the Web site. I am fortunate enough to have met Mr. Jim Kennedy of Kennedy Fine Art, a giant in the art world, who has opened many doors for me. I still hope to someday open a quaint little art gallery in a city that shares my love of art. For now, though, the point is to never give up. One additional topic I wish to touch on before making my summation is something known as a "buyout" offer. In truth, I'd completed the chapter, when a recent news story focused on the Ford Motor Company's current offer to some employees. So, realizing this could affect my readers, I wish to share my thoughts on buyouts.

Generally, in police work, buyouts would be offered to seventeen-year officers if the normal retirement is at twenty years. I don't know how common buyout offers are in departments around the country (or even Florida), but I have heard that it's a good deal for the officer. Basically, the seventeen-year officer is offered an immediate twenty-year (full) pension if he or she agrees to retire when the offer is made. The city gains, because they are shedding the higher-echelon salaries by pensioning the seventeen-year officers off. For the officer, it means (to me) three free years: an early release, if you will. My city does not as of yet implement such buyouts, but they're reportedly considering it. Financially speaking, cities are said to benefit from buyouts, because with the money they save paying such senior officers, they can hire two rookie officers for about the same price. In my opinion, buyouts would only not be best for officers who have definitely decided to stay past twenty years. Regarding departments that require twenty-five (or more) years of service for retirement, I don't know at what year a buyout offer would be tendered. Additionally, for officers who plan to stay on the job after their normal retirement date a D.R.O.P. (Deferred Retirement Option Plan) plan should be considered. My department does not offer a D.R.O.P. plan, so I cannot speak in detail about it. But in essence, the plan (usually five years) is a contract wherein the officer agrees to retire at the end of those five additional years, and a portion of his or her salary is laid aside, to boost the officer's pension. I am sure I am oversimplifying this, but that's how it basically operates. Consult your payroll department for information on buyout offers and D.R.O.P. programs as to whether they are offered.

In closing, then, it's my hope that after reading my book, you're now headed in the right direction. I stress that I am not certified in financial planning. That lack of title, however, does not preclude me from offering you helpful advice that has worked for me, and worked well. I stand by the education provided to me by my alma mater and by a wealth of experiences amassed over the course of a career doing the job you now do. By following the ideas put forth in this book, I have managed to successfully retire as a young man, financially secure. I believe you can do the same if you get moving and stick to it. Prove me right.

Epilogue

The world is a very different place in the fourteen years that have passed since I handed over those first dollars to my mom toward saving, and now, in 2007 at the commencement of this book's publishing.

Wars, natural disasters, economic rallies and slumps—and for me, too many good-byes. I lost my parents, who guided me with love and support all my life. Their belief in my strength and ability gave me the courage to pursue my inspiration. During this book's writing I came across a quote from the noted author James Baldwin (1924-1987) who said, "One writes out of one thing only, one's own experience. Everything depends on how relentlessly one forces from this experience the last drop, sweet or bitter, it can possibly give."

It occurred to me in those great words that I had passed the litmus test set forth by Mr. Baldwin. Whether inspired or mundane, this is my experience, my story. I still live by my words; still working and saving but most of all, still planning. The only difference is that without my beloved parents, it's been a bittersweet journey. I once asked my mom, a long time ago, why she had me. She replied, "I brought you into the world to help others," and smiled. Although I am still sometimes moved to tears when I recall these tender words, perhaps I can smile in the thought that I may help you.

About the Author

The small, working-class town in New Jersey I grew up in is known as Carteret. I completed Carteret High School in 1977, and then attended Middlesex County College in Edison, New Jersey, where I earned an Associate of Science degree in criminal justice. I've always had a bent for scholastics, and while at Middlesex, I was one of only two criminology students chosen to set up the library at the new (Middlesex County) police academy going up on campus at the time (1980). Also, while at Middlesex, I was inducted into Phi Beta Kappa (National College Honor Society).

I relocated to Florida with my family in late 1983 and, armed with an A.S. degree and many dreams, I entered the Pinellas Police Academy in the spring of 1984, graduating third in my class, as a State of Florida certified police officer late that summer.

I then began as a rookie police officer one week after graduating the academy, on the Belleair (Florida) Police Department. *Hogan Knows Best* was filmed in Belleair (until the Hogans relocated). Thirteen months later, I left Belleair P.D. to accept a position as a recruit police officer on the Clearwater (Florida) Police Department. There, I served as patrol officer until retiring in 2003. During this time period, I earned a Bachelor of Arts degree in criminology at St. Leo College, graduating summa cum laude, in 1992.

Afterward, I did some graduate work at the University of South Florida.

Always the idealist and romantic, I wrote two noteworthy poems: "Ode to Jenny" and "Remembrances of Karen," which were published in anthologies by the National Library of Poetry, in 1995 and 1996, respectively. "Ode" took third prize in a national amateur open poetry contest in 1995.

I'm also a Master Freemason (Star Lodge #69 F. & A.M., Largo, Florida) and a U.S. Coast Guard licensed captain (Port: Miami, Florida). I've always kept in mind and close to my heart those lessons imparted to me by my grandfather, O. Harry Orlando, and my wonderful parents, Frederick and Barbara: to always do the right thing and to lead an upright life.

I never imagined writing a book. The experience seemed more like one of mentoring from afar; perhaps offering to you something you may find useful. As far as whether I'm qualified to do so, only *you* can say.

Printed in the United States
100845LV00001B/96/A